The Truth Is...

The moments of motherhood that make

a Mother

Best Wishes!
Hannah Madsen

Hannah J. Madsen

ISBN Paperback: 979-8-9851171-2-7

Digital: 979-8-9851171-3-4

LCCN: 2022914677

Cover design by Jevgenija Bitter

Interior Design by Rozie Marshall

Photography by Kelsey Minnick, Ph.D.

Printed in the United States of America

CW Publishing LLC, Castle Rock Colorado

For information on special discounts for bulk purchases, please contact CW Publishing LLC, at codie@Codiewinslow.com or hannahjmadsen@gmail.com

Some names and identifying details of people described in this book have been altered to protect their privacy.

An important note: This book is not intended as a substitute for the medical recommendation of physicians or other health-care providers. Rather, it is intended to offer information to help the reader cooperate with physicians and health professionals in a mutual quest for optimum well-being. The identities of people described in the case histories have been changed to protect patient confidentiality. The publisher and the author are not responsible for any goods and/or services offered or referred to in this book and expressly disclaim all liability in connection with the fulfillment of orders for any such goods and/or services and for any damage, loss, or expense to person or property arising out of or relating to them.

Contents

Dedication

To the real MVP, my husband. Shawn, without your love, encouragement, and support, this project would have never seen completion. Thank you isn't enough.

To my family. Mom, Dad, and my brother, Logan. You all have given me the best that life has had to offer since childhood. I thank all three of you for a firm foundation to grow upon, and the world's largest safety net to fall into when I fail. You three are the reason I am brave. Thank you.

To my girls. Your love changed me as a person. I never knew love like ours could exist. Thank you for being my entire world. The pages of this book wouldn't have been filled without you and your wonderful hearts. Stay wild my beautiful girls, life is more fun that way.

Dear Beautiful Reader,

Have you ever woken up covered in spit up from the infant you're not supposed to be bed sharing with? Or a toddler standing next to your bed who not only leaked pee out of her diaper, but also has poop smeared up the back of her pajamas? Me too. It happens to moms. No matter how pretty, put together, organized or chaotic we are, shit happens, quite literally. I am a woman who loved her life before children. I was selfish with my time and completely adored my husband. I must say I still do, it's just different now. When I had children, everything changed. I often find myself feeling alone, or crazy. Or have thoughts of, "this can't possibly be happening to other people...right?" Know this, you are not the only one who has removed cheerios from the back of your pants when you stand up because your toddler was having a sharp shooting competition with your butt crack. I'm going through it too.

I want you to begin to see how God can show up in really funny moments of motherhood. These moments are what make a mother. He often shows up for me when I'm on my knees cleaning barfed up milk with tears streaming down my face. And He shows up when I shout at my toddler about the stupidest obscenely priced $15 pack of bubbles I've ever seen, that is now dumped out on my back patio. The point is, He always shows up.

When I first became a mama, I felt like I was wearing a belt that was three sizes too small that I was destined to wear for the rest of my life. I was suffocating. Prior to having children, moms across the nation talked to me about how amazingly wonderful motherhood is and how glorious this was and how special that was. Well, I'm sorry but I call bullshit. Although many of these things may be true in freeze frame moments of life, they are not the reality for me every day. Everyday moments for me looked like cracked nipples, a scar from hip to hip, and a screaming infant that I was in no way equipped to care for. It was a battle. I was terrified and was definitely not overjoyed in motherhood bliss.

I had a thought. I wonder if other moms struggle like me? I wonder if other moms feel like this? Do they have a support system like I do? What if they didn't? This thought kept me up at night. My heart ached for the struggling moms with nowhere to turn. Tears streamed knowing that somewhere, someone was feeling so isolated and alone from becoming a mother and there was nothing that I could do about it. So, I wrote. I wrote down all of my stories and feelings and all about my journey of becoming a mama. I wanted that mama to find a friend. If my book reaches one sad or lonely mom and comforts her in any way, then my goal has been reached. This book is not for notoriety or money, it's truly to help my mama peers feel less like throwing themselves off the deck. Albeit a tall order, we can work through this mess of motherhood together.

I started writing this book when my oldest was 6 months old and am finishing it when she is three years old. Since that time, we have welcomed another little girl, who is about to turn two. Whoa. If these stories seem a little too real at moments, it's because they are. I am in the low down, dirty trenches of being a mom just like you. I am struggling, just like you. I am terrified of being responsible for the next generation, just like you. I am an everyday regular mom trying to make a difference in this crazy world we live in. Who knows, maybe it'll work. Maybe, just maybe, I'll make a difference for you.

This book is laid out in four sections full of small stories and lessons I've learned. Some of them barely by the skin of my teeth. Each section has its purpose and is different than the last. Being a mother who is in the trenches myself, I know you can't read long chapters. Who has the time, am I right? I've broken down big lessons and long stories into bite size chapters packed with a punch. Take each chapter like you used to take shots in college; quickly, efficiently, and effectively. I want you, my reader, to be able to pick up my book when you're really struggling and read an encouraging chapter in less than five minutes. We don't always have time to sit and chat for hours at a time, I know. My book is designed with you in mind, and with you in my heart.

We grow as humans when we become moms. It's hard, and wonderful, and awful. It's smelly, terrible, hilarious, confusing, and all together chaos; but I love it. I love every moment with my two beautiful daughters and wouldn't change any of it for anything. I want you to know that you can exist in both of these opposite worlds at once. It's ok to Google if Grandma and Grandpa can temporarily take custody of these snot monsters, and also not want to let go of a hug so they can play at the park. Both exist in the life of a mother. Both feelings are real, intense, and extremely valid. To be honest, I'm here for it. I think it is such a wild ride to become a mom. I want you to find a friend in my words. Through these chapters, I want you to feel supported and less alone. This stuff truly does happen to everyone. Every single mother has indeed at one point in time wiped snot off of their child's nose with their bare hand and wiped it on their pants; I promise. I want you to begin to learn to laugh at yourself and learn to enjoy the small moments in motherhood that truly make you as strong as a mother.

Sincerely,

Hannah

X

Part One:

Relate

"The truth is, I wasn't born to fit in. I was born to
go my own way and blaze my own trail. I was
already born enough. I don't need the validation
from girls, at any age, to give me identity. God did
that for me on the cross."

Friendships and relationships are such an important part of our everyday lives. We are created as social beings and have the innate need for connection. When we become mothers, this task becomes twenty times as hard. We become isolated in our own lives and more and more lonely over time. Our friends and social priorities slip away, heck we even allow ourselves to slip away. Relating to others and building friendships are two things in motherhood I wish I had known more about before becoming a parent. I wish I had known how important it was to have a tribe, and how devastatingly hard it is to create and maintain it. So here I am. I want all mamas to have a friend. Even if we can't be friends in person, I hope that my words serve as a comfort to you in the times that you need it most. I hope that my heart laid out for you on these pages serves as a connection for you.

Hi, I'm Hannah and I am an overworked, exhausted mama just trying to find the joy in parenthood. Whenever I have been a part of a friend group (or mom clan), it's because I relate in some way to the other people involved. I can relate to the way they parent, or speak, or use humor. Or even relate to the fact that, no matter how we do things, we both acknowledge we are completely and utterly clueless. That last category makes up most of my friend group. For example, when I look at my best friends, it is comical to see how different we are. We differ in looks, financial statuses, motherhood experiences, likes, dislikes etc. So why the heck are we friends?! It comes down to the ability to relate to people even when we are different. I relate to their constant positivity, huge hearts, and available shoulders to cry on. I can relate to my friend Jeana's financial savvy and my friend Taylor's ability to speak the truth (at all costs). I can relate to my friend Crystal's ability to put a rambunctious toddler's needs above her own, and my friend Megan's ability to bring a community of mothers together. I can relate to my friend Amber's constant search for knowledge and her full dedication to her marriage. All six of us are incredibly different, but the thing that brings us together is our ability to relate to one another in very significant ways.

In this section of the book, I want to show you, my heart. Who I am, how I parent, my ups and downs, my triumphs and my pitfalls. I want you to see that I don't have it all together, and hopefully you can (at a bare minimum), relate to that. I want you to read all of the most memorable moments and see that we are more similar than different. I want to come along side you in the journey of motherhood and be your friend. I want to share my life with you so you can see that the grass is not always greener in another mom's yard. Here are some fun facts about me. Hopefully you can relate, and we can be friends.

I love Jesus

I have two little girls

I am a midwestern girl living in Colorado

I hate spiders

I love soda

I call it soda

I absolutely adore my husband

I love the outdoors

I am working on my potty mouth

I am an outgoing introvert

I love playing with my kids (when I'm not tired of course)

I get overwhelmed easily

I thought being a mom was going to be easier than this

I would still choose my girls, knowing what I know now

I probably need therapy

I desire deeper friendships rather than acquaintances

I procrastinate like it's a job

I have self-doubt and self-confidence simultaneously

I try my absolute very best on a daily basis

I am completely winging this motherhood thing.

Chapter One

Can't Get It Back

The truth is... I can't change the past, and that's ok.

I became a mama in November of 2018, when I learned I was pregnant with my first. My husband and I had been trying for so long, and until this point were unsuccessful, no matter what we tried.

I was working as a hair stylist at the time, and we had just bought a new house (which was a fixer upper). Life was always in full force and in fast motion. We were madly in love and insanely busy.

Due to stress, I had an eye twitch that wouldn't go away. After the third week passed, I began googling. It said anything lasting more than 10 days, see your doctor. So, I made the appointment. My doc and I laughed at the stupid twitch, as it made looking at me quite funny. She said she had medication to help but saw in my chart I've been trying to have a baby. She asked if there was any chance, I could be pregnant (because of the side effects of the medication). I said 'no' and explained our difficulty conceiving. She agreed to prescribe me the medication and said to take an at home test just to be sure, because the medicine could hurt a baby. Will do doc. I picked up the medicine from the pharmacy and then headed to Walmart to get a test. I grabbed a cheap one and conveniently had to pee. I took the test in a Walmart bathroom just to be sure I wasn't pregnant.

My husband and I had become pregnant once before, about six months prior to that. It resulted in a miscarriage that shook me to my core. I did a huge pregnancy reveal to my husband with a daddy book and all. I videoed the whole thing so we could always remember the moment. It was precious. But the pregnancy never developed. It broke my heart. I add this to show you that I truly do love special reveals. I love recording special moments that you can never get back. I wanted the memory.

As the second pink line showed up in the Walmart stall, I almost fainted. I was so sure that I wasn't pregnant; I never even planned for the possibility that I was. There was no special video, no beautiful moment with my husband. I was alone, in a Walmart bathroom stall. I was devastated that this would forever and always be my story. I will also admit that I leave this part out of the story most of the time because, honestly, who would this happen to?! Who would do that?! Me. I did.

I am a perfectionist down to my soul. I want things to be perfect. I always have, and I fear I always will. I wanted this moment to be wrapped up in a pretty pink bow complete with confetti and a song in the background. I wanted sweet, innocent, expectant, and happy. Instead, I got a Walmart bathroom. Alone. With an eye twitch.

I rushed back to my doctor and told her the news. I could no longer take the medication she prescribed but we did figure out the eye twitch. It was due to the stress on my body. It went away after about 12 weeks of pregnancy, but boy was it annoying.

Driving home from the doctor's office, so many thoughts raced through my mind, but mostly how in the hell was I going to tell my husband that we had done it? Well, he knew we had done IT, but how was I going to break it to him that this time we were successful. I am very self-aware, and I know what my face looks like, especially when I'm feeling any type of emotion. I often must ask my face to use its inside voice, because wow, it's brutal. I knew he would know the moment I walked through the door that something was up.

I opened our door and heard him fussing in the kitchen. My face immediately flushed red. I walk towards him, and he sees me. Game over. "What's wrong?!" he immediately asks. "Well, we found out what was causing the twitch…" "Yeah?" "Well, I um… I'm… the thing is… Ok, well I'm pregnant." There it was. I said it. This beautiful, special, life changing news all crumbled together and fumbling out of my mouth. It wasn't the announcement I wanted. It wasn't special. I was sad. I began to cry, and he was so confused, I could tell. Men. I blurted through tears that I had ruined everything! "I found out in a WALMART BATHROOM!!" He was even more confused as I had left that bit of the story out. He pulled me close, walked me to our couch and sat me on his lap. He requested I back up and start from the beginning. I told him the whole saga and how upset I was.

Laughter snuck out of him. He beamed with joy, and said he was so excited for us. He reminded me that we weren't perfect people, and our story is full of funny moments just like this, and that he wouldn't have had it any other way. He loved it. He loved me.

Life isn't wrapped up in a pretty bow all the time. No matter how hard we try to control everything, sometimes things happen. This whole thing went so unexpectedly that it was actually kind of funny. Little did I know at the time that it would be a theme for me throughout motherhood. It's not perfect. It can't be wrapped in a pretty bow. There are ups and downs everywhere on your journey, but it is still real and raw and hysterically funny. I wouldn't have it any other way.

I had so many plans for a perfect motherhood journey. I had cute pregnancy announcements and gender reveals. You name the occasion, and I had a plan. Looking back, I can see from the very beginning I was going to learn a much-needed lesson. I can't control everything, and if I try to (or if I get devastated anytime things go awry), I will miss it. I will miss the beautiful imperfection of motherhood that makes it completely worth it.

Don't miss it, mama. Choose to let go and take it as it comes. You will be ok, I promise.

Although this is the first story of this book, I want to reflect back to the introduction. Remember when I told you I'm not perfect? Remember when I said we can be friends because we are more similar than different? I meant it. Wholeheartedly. Although this book is full of real-life mama moments that brought me to my knees and humbled me to my core just like this one, it's also full of lessons I've learned along the way. I have made it through every story and have lived to tell the tale. There is no judgement here, just pure aggressive honesty, and a weary hand extended in friendship.

Chapter Two

But This Mouth

The truth is... But this MOUTH!!!

The truth is, I want to relate to moms. I want to build a community of support around everyone who needs it. I remember being a new mom myself and feeling so often that I just didn't have the energy to sugar coat things anymore. I wasn't magical mommy, and I wasn't a polished woman, and it took physical energy to pretend. I found myself gravitating towards ladies who spoke it as it was. The words of our conversations often came out harsh and a little rough around the edges, but they were real. Apologies were many times given to the group after our conversations for the rawness. Abundant grace was always given as we all knew exactly how the other mama was feeling, and she deserved a safe place to vent. So do you and I.

I brought a new friend I had met at a church function to a mommy playdate with some friends. I was excited to see both of my worlds combined. I love bringing women together and creating friendships, it makes me happy. We began to watch as our littles play on the slides and swing from the monkey bars.

About 10 or 15 minutes passed and gone were all the hellos and the nice to meet You's. In came the real grit of our friendships. We started talking about life as we saw it. What was happening in our homes and who had offended us or betrayed our trust. Some talked about their husbands, and I spilled the beans about what life with a newborn seriously looked like. So many colorful words filled the air it probably looked similar to sinful confetti. I hadn't realized that this may have offended my new friend. She may not have been used to this. She was soft-spoken and kind. She certainly didn't belong in the Navy like my friends and I.

We got back to the car, and I immediately apologized for the words she just had to endure. I apologized for our harshness and tried to explain the therapeutic effects of our word vomit. To my surprise she stopped me mid-apology and said she really had a good time. She said she was so happy to be with real people, who loved Jesus, and had real world troubles. She asked to join us again next week, because she had some stuff to get off her chest. She didn't want to dive in on the first meeting for fear we would think she was the crazy one. Did you hear that? She was worried we would think SHE was crazy. No girl, you're completely normal. You have feelings, emotions, troubles, and complaints. That is the norm. She returned week after week for the friendships and honesty of the group, and she is still my friend to this day.

I want to create that space for us as well. I want you to hear me as I speak. Let me begin by saying I love Jesus with my whole heart, and I strive to be more like Him every day... BUT THIS MOUTH!! I pray every day that the good Lord Jesus breaks me of these chains because my feelings can't help but come out in curse words sometimes. My father was in the military, which in terms of language, if you know, you know. It isn't pretty.

I will never use the Lord's name in vain, and I will rarely drop an F-bomb, surely not in print, but heavens to Betsy if I don't use other less offensive and very colorful words. I'm human. I sin and I'm embarrassed about it most of the time, but that's me. I want you to know ME, hear ME. The real version of me doesn't shout, "What in the heavens happened in here my sweet darling girl?!" The real version of me shouts steaming hot words that my kids should never hear me say - words that I'm not even allowed to say in church. I don't want you to walk away from my words with the polished, watered-down version of Hannah. Where is the fun in that?

You, my friend, deserve a mom group like mine. A group in which you can be completely and authentically you. Build a group of friends who are God-fearing, loving, and hilarious women who encourage you on the daily. And find women who forgive quickly because motherhood gets messy.

So, as you read my words, please extend grace. I am writing this book in my mess, in the trenches of motherhood happening in real-time. I want to be as genuine as possible, and sometimes a mommy just needs to curse, worse shit has happened. My heart is never to offend, but to let you behind the curtain of my heart and see me for who I truly am. I am wild, funny, fierce, scared, traumatized, talented, loved, and chosen... but this mouth.

Chapter Three

Colic

The truth is.... my kid was diagnosed with colic.

My sweet and beautiful girl never stopped crying. She couldn't sleep alone, or on her back, and refused to be put down. I was tired and felt so helpless. I thought motherhood was going to be different than that. Wasn't it supposed to be beautiful and filled with endless hours of snuggling and smelling my newborn's head? Wasn't I supposed to be happy? At least that's what people told me. They told me all about the sweet hours that passed while your warm soft baby slept in your arms. Where the hell was that? If people were only able to peek behind my curtain, they would see hours of screaming and a crying mama. However, I didn't want others to know that; they might have judged me. They might have thought I was doing a bad job, or worse, that I was a bad mom.

I posted beautiful pictures of my girl on social media because that's how my heart sees her, but she wasn't always sunshine. There had been endless storms in the long hours of the night. Hours that seemed to take months to pass by. Hours that caused physical pain to my body as I paced the floors of my home. She cried because she couldn't help it, and so did I.

I write this as a reality check. I posted cute pictures because I love my daughter, I really do. However, moms out there need to know that between those snapshots are countless tears from her and me, snappy comments made out of frustration to my spouse and long showers that would drown out the screams. Facebook is not reality. Reality is me calling my mom at six AM begging and sobbing for help, and her showing up as fast as her car will drive. Reality is trying every doctor recommended, Google suggested and WebMD solution out there. Reality is feeling like I was failing. Also, the reality is that this is completely and utterly untrue. Moms are always their hardest critic and if you're like me you can point out every flaw and shortcoming.

I wanted to yell and ask, "Why me?!" I wanted to host my own pity party and most of all, I wanted to be angry. But that's not what my sweet daughter needed. She needed love. I wanted to love my baby with a happy heart. God gave me my daughter because He knew I could love her through her pain and our cries. He knew I was always meant to be her mommy and her my little peanut. It's not easy, but it's my story and it's beautiful all the same.

We are not alone. Many mothers out there suffer in silence, and I choose not to be one of them. I hope you don't either. I choose to speak up and ask for support during a time in my life that is testing me, and I pray that you do as well mama. If you're a colic child survivor, let's chat! Having a colic child is a whole different playing field in which the team is stacked against you and the rules aren't fair. I promise, if you are going through this, it will pass. There is nothing that will cure it. There is no easy answer, except for time. I know, I know. Those are the worst and most cruel words that can be spoken to a mother dealing with colic, but unfortunately, they are true.

What's also true is that you will make it, and you will be stronger for it. You will have much more patience than ever before and a much deeper bond with the child. You two together will overcome a huge challenge and when you are on the other side, your relationship will be unbreakable. There is light at the end of this long tunnel mama, you just have to get there, and you most certainly can.

Chapter Four

Glitter

The truth is... we need to talk about glitter.

There are two types of people in this world - those who love glitter, and the sane. If you love glitter, turn the page, I'll pray for you.

I had a thought. The devil uses lies and deceit to cause God's people to stray. We all recognize most sins and lies when presented in everyday life. And like a good Christian, we steer clear. Am I right?! So how did glitter sneak past this defense? Satan himself says glitter is so pretty and sparkly and fun!! It's the best according to him. I'm here as a humble servant of God to call out glitter for what it actually is. Glitter is cornea ripping sin dust. I said it. Fight me. It gets everywhere.

When I say everywhere I truly mean it. I will be changing my toddler's diaper weeks after Grandma allowed glitter at her house, and I'm still wiping it out of her butt crack. Why it's in her butt crack is another question altogether, but nonetheless it's there.

It's in the hair, under the nails, between the cracks, up the noses, on the tongues, and is now a permanent part of everyone's skin. Feel free to freak out now. You will forever resemble Glitter Troll. Not feeling so sparkly? The glitter from last week's art project doesn't care... it's still holding on shining brighter than ever. Now just like most sin, there is a false upside. My daughter's poop is delightful. It's sparkly and always changing colors. However, this upside is not enough to outweigh the constant eyeball scratching, glitter snot, and glue dust that my daughter loves oh so deeply.

If you like glitter, you need to pray for forgiveness. That's all.

No dreams were killed in the making of this opinion.

Chapter Five

My Best Sucked

The truth is... my best sucked.

Where do I begin? Have you ever been in a season of life that is so crazy you have to literally stop your body from moving, take an audibly deep breath, choke back tears and watch all 107 balls you've been juggling hit the ground? Some even hit you on the way down. The metaphorical ball of being a good employee... bam, on the ground. A good friend, smash. A person with good hygiene? Well, let's be honest, that ball fell a long while ago. In the early days of being a mother, everything around me was crumbling, and somehow, I was doing my very best. Here's the deal, my best sucked. My best hadn't always sucked, and it won't always continue to suck. Sometimes I think God used a tennis racquet to spike smash things to the ground because I was so incredibly stubborn, I thought I could do it all. I needed to get an umbrella because I was bruised y'all. I was tired and hurt. I was 'failing'. Although that was an awfully hard space to be in, here's what I learned.

Could it be possible that God was trying to get my attention? Could it be possible that He was trying to get my reliance? And could it be possible that He wanted me back at the foot of the cross in His mercy? I'm thinking yes. I try so damn hard to handle this life on my own. In the deepest parts of my heart, I want to be a good mom, wife, friend, etc. The list goes on, and on, and on. I want to make everyone around me happy. I want to make people laugh and give good advice and bring you coffee when you need it and take care of my kids and be a stellar wife and volunteer in the community, and, and, and. And it's enough. My best efforts continually fell short in the days after I became a mom. My best just kind of sucked.

Here's the good news. God's efforts for my happiness and for my life never suck. Not even one time. Not even a little. He is constantly there leading me back to His arms. So, here I sit. I sit in the waiting and in the hurt. I sit in the defeat and sorrow of my own efforts. I sit because I know He shows up in these moments, and He brings clarity to my life when I look to Him. Just sucks that it takes such defeat to get there. If you're like me, here's a tailor-made PSA. Slow down. Remember that it isn't about you or the 107 tennis balls you're trying to juggle. It's about Him, it always has been. Also, if you refuse to listen to His call like me, get an umbrella (and some safety goggles), because when God chooses to hammer-smash things to the ground for you, they don't fall tenderly. They come crashing, and they hurt. Armor up, put on your big girl undies and do absolutely nothing. That's right, stop. Stop trying to do God's job. Stop trying to rule your own life as if it belongs to you. Stop the control. He's got you. He always has. He also has a mean right spike, so take notice and get a strong umbrella. He will always provide you with one. Also, learn the words, "I'm sorry", and "help". He likes those. A little tip from me to you, "I can do it on my own…" has never gone well for me. My own sucks. My best sucks. Please send snacks.

Chapter Six

I Was Left Out

The truth is... I was left out.

Growing up I never felt invited or enough, and I definitely never fit in.

In Elementary school, I remember asking myself for the first time, "Is it me? Why don't they like me?" The popular girls would all play on the bars during recess. They would talk about their birthday parties and the grand plans they had coming up. I was never invited. I remember going so far as inviting myself to their parties in hopes their mom would make them invite me. I just wanted friends.

I asked the question again when what seemed like every girl in the 9th grade got asked to the Homecoming dance by a boy, and I had to do the asking. To make matters worse, my date left me sitting alone at dinner while he walked to the grocery store because he was bored. I wanted to be like everyone else, I wanted a kind date. I didn't deserve what I got, a solo dinner before my first high school dance.

Recently, I asked the question again, when I saw pictures of someone who I thought was a close friend going to concerts and events with other ladies, but I wasn't invited. At 34 years old, I hate to admit it, but I asked again, "Why am I never enough? Why don't I fit in? Why don't I get invited? Why aren't I like everyone else?!"

It's so incredibly painful to be an outsider with big ideas. It's hurtful to be different from everyone else and be left out because of it. I'm sure if I wore the same clothes and listened to the same music, or even had the same political beliefs, I would have gotten invited, but that's not me. I was never willing to change myself to get an invite. So many tears have fallen, that I've become used to being left behind.

Being a not-by-choice loner, you can imagine how terrified I was of motherhood. Everyone says, "It takes a village." Well crap, because I had three friends, two of which lived out of state, and my mom. That's it. I must add that I have about the best husband that God ever created. Seriously ladies, be jealous. However, he can only do so much for the part of my heart that needs a village. The part that desperately needs a mom friend.

What if I'm a loner mom? What if my girls notice that? What's my answer to that? Will my apparent ability to repel other women hurt my children? How can it be different for my kids? How can I get them invited? What if…? How will…? Why me…? Anyone else been on this ridiculously unhealthy downward spiral toward the depths? I thought as much.

Here's the thing, I'm not being left behind. I just had to birth my best friends. I had to be patient. I'm thriving as a mom. The truth is, I wasn't born to fit in. I was born to go my own way and blaze my own trail. I was already born enough. I don't need the validation from girls, at any age, to give me identity. God did that for me on the cross.

I almost let fear stop me from creating life. I almost let my uniqueness inhibit my desire for children. How twisted is that? I wonder how many young women are in this exact same position? I wonder how many moms still feel left out? I would wager to bet, quite a few.

Shift your perspective. You gave birth to some pretty awesome besties. Your children. Sure, they are frenemies at best most days, but they are there. They adore you. They need you. You are strong enough to be a mom, with or without a plethora of friendships. You will never again be left out, at least not for another 18 years or so.

If all else fails and your children don't want to be your friend either (because they may not want to be), remember there is always me. I'm here for you, mama. I am rooting for you. You don't need tons of friends, you just need a select few who understand your heart. If you don't fit in, that's ok, because maybe you were never meant to, like me. Maybe, just maybe you were created to blaze your own trail and be the change you want to see in this world.

Chapter Seven

No Idea

The truth is... I have no idea what I'm doing.

Becoming a mother is like being cast in the lead role in a musical when you can't sing, weren't given the script, and you're put on stage opening night.... go for it girl. Ugh, okee dokee... "Let it goooo... let it goooo". Even though I have no clue what I'm doing a solid 85.7% of the time, the show must go on. Motherhood is a trip.

I remember one morning, my 1 1/2-year-old straight looked me in my soul, grunted, slapped her booty and said, "poop". I've never been so proud of my parenting. What I'm doing is working. I was straight up excited for her communication and comprehension.

Now ladies and gentlemen, I remember not so long ago being pissed at the thought of a friend soiling their pants, but today, today I clapped and cheered. Then stood in awkward silence pondering my actions. Thoughts flooded me like waves of suppressed emotion... "Who am I? Did I just seriously cheer for a now smooshed turd in my daughter's butt? Holy wow I am different. Does my husband like the new me? Does my kid like me? Did my reaction scare her? She's staring at me... say something... can she tell I'm having an internal meltdown? Why am I melting down over poop? Do I need a therapist? Pull it together, woman!"

After I cheered, pondered my life, and possibly scarred my child with my awkward silence, I changed her diaper and gave her a snack. Ya know, just killin' the mom game. If you don't know what you're doing as a mother, it's ok. If you feel like the only way to emotionally un-scar your child from your internal monologue is to change their poop and give them a snack, that's normal... hopefully. I think it's ok to give yourself grace. We also need to give ourselves the opportunity to process how different our lives are now. Things we once thought incomprehensible happen on the daily. Things that we swore would never happen to us, do. We need a second to recognize that, and I dare say more than a moment to grow from it. The most important thing is to just keep mommin' because, ma'am, they don't need perfection; they need you. All 8,876 crazy layers of YOU. Also, if this has scarred you, go poop and get a snack. You'll feel better.

Chapter Eight

The Sass

The truth is... I birthed a sassier version of myself, and I'm sorry.

Cher once said she tattooed her butt and she's sorry. Fair. My life's catch phrase is a bit different. *I was sassy to my mom and I'm sorry!* Mom always warned me that I was going to have a baby "just like me". God must really favor my mother because He sprinkled on the extra sass on my beautiful second born.

She's just like me and I'm sorry!

As I was talking to God, I found myself bartering with Him about the sass level of my children as if I could somehow make it easier on myself. The only thing I could hear in return is a chuckle and, "Oh dear sweet daughter of mine, you ain't seen nothing yet...". Despite the fact that God used the word ain't (yes, I'm shocked as well), I knew His statement was true. After I went to the bathroom and wiped the poo out of my pants, because y'all I was terrified, I sat in silence. I sat reflecting on my day and how my toddler straight up gave me the silent treatment. I reflected more so on how much it hurt me. When my sweet, beautiful ball of happiness and fun wouldn't even look at me, my heart broke. What happens when she's older and means what she says? All girls sass their mom, we're human. How do we as mothers not fall to pieces when that happens? Do you all have private snack and tissue stashes randomly around the house so you can sneak away and bawl in private while stuffing your face with Reese's? I'll add that to my to-do list because if this kind of thing continues, I'm going to need it. Side note: she gave me the cold shoulder because I made her sit down in her stroller. I know, I'm a monster.

Many of my memories are of my mother and our relationship throughout the years. All the things I could have (and probably should have) done differently are always on my mind. I'm so glad that I'm given the chance to make it right by giving her a Grandchild that is exactly like me. Well, two actually. I provide the comic relief she's been waiting for all these 34 years. It's rightfully deserved, but Jesus-take-the-wheel. Mother, sit back and relax with your well-earned popcorn and enjoy the laughter... because "Mama, you ain't seen nothin yet…"

If you're finding yourself in the same spot - evaluating how you treated your own mother and hilariously regretting it - I have some advice. Talk to your mom. Whether you're a lucky one and she is still on Earth with you, or if she is up in Heaven, have a chat. Tell her all the things you are learning now and all the childhood memories that make you laugh. Thank her for being her. I also recommend asking for her help. She's walked this path before you and I guarantee she has some of the most solid advice there is to give. Ladies, love your mama. Whether near or far, she will always be the only one you have.

Chapter Nine

The Truth Is Scary

The truth is... the truth is scary.

I was out shopping at Target for the necessities (insert eye roll here) when I ran into a pregnant mom to be in the pajama aisle. She saw my girls in the cart and said, "Goodness, you've got your hands full, I can't wait!" as she rubbed her tummy. We struck up conversation about pregnancy, and the challenges, and how excited she was to be a mom to her soon-to-be born little girl. I forced a smile and probably had the look of sheer panic all over my face.

Here's the deal, no one told me. No one told me how hard motherhood actually is. No one told me that often times it feels like this never-ending challenge with blow after blow, without any rest. Victories and awesome moments can be so few and far between that you can feel like a failure for weeks at a time. No one told me how bad my heart would hurt when my babies cried and how much my heart would ache for the relationship I once had with my husband.

Becoming a mother puts you out on a deserted island alone for some time until your babies grow a little older and you can rejoin society. It's the hardest thing to go through and no one told me the truth about it. The fact that no one told me truly makes my blood boil and when I think about it too long, I get angry.

I looked at my new friend in the aisle of Target and said, "You're going to be a great mom and it's worth every tear." She thanked me and we went about our shopping in separate directions. I was truly haunted by this interaction. I had done what so many mothers before me had done. I sugar-coated it. I felt as if I had betrayed her. I almost ran after her to tell her the truth about being a mom, but I'm glad I didn't because security probably would have been called. Could you imagine a mom with two babies in her cart chasing after a pregnant lady screaming, "IT'S ALL A LIE!!! IT'S AWFUL!! THEY DEFECATE EVERYWHERE!!!!" Yea, me neither. So instead of becoming that lady, I took time to think about why I hadn't said something else.

I didn't tell her, because although all the terrible things are true, so are the good things. When my girls hug me, it's like no other feeling I've ever had, ever. When they finally learn a lesson and do something correctly, the pride that swells in my heart for them is all-consuming. When that little twinkle in their eye makes contact with mine during a fit of laughter, I happy cry. I love my girls to the depth of my being, and so will she. She will live for the moments of pure bliss that I thought were other worldly before becoming a mama. She will stare into her little girls' eyes and know without a shadow of a doubt that she is exactly where she needs to be. I didn't tell her the full truth because I knew, although the truth is very real in motherhood, we can overcome all of it because of the love in our hearts. She IS going to be a fantastic mom, and her journey IS going to be hard. Those two things exist at the same dang time, and who am I to pop someone's happy bubble? The emotions of motherhood are earned. It's a rite of passage. It's a club with an impossibly high entrance fee asking us to sacrifice it all. Sacrifice is scary, but the reward is more than worth it. I promise.

Chapter Ten

Waking Up Sucks

The truth is... Waking up sucks.

Sleep is a unicorn.

Waking up is hard. It's almost impossible because it is almost certainly followed by a sleepless night. I'm a mom. Sleep is like the journey to find a horse with a horn on its head. It doesn't exist. It's a flipping unicorn.

Mornings usually start with a crying baby or two. After bouts of crying and indistinguishable yelling, there is silence. "Did they go back to sleep?" I think to myself as I freeze stiff as a board in bed. After a few moments pass, my body relaxes a bit and I roll over to enjoy this extended sleep time as I know it won't last long. After what seems like 30 seconds, I hear my kid's footsteps near the side of my bed. "Hi mama," my daughter whispers as she crawls up and pulls my eyelids open one at a time. Through bloodshot and weary eyes, I always reply, "Good morning sweet girl".

My beautiful daughters are 17 months apart and do their best to assist me with waking up on time. No alarm clock needed. I lay there for a moment before standing up to help the girls. I wonder if God is punking me. I wonder if my mother paid God off for all the times when I was "bored" and woke her up at the crack of dawn just for someone to talk to. I realize now that payback is rightly deserved.

I used to love sleep. I loved how my blankets hugged me and let me escape. Drift off to a lovely place void of all of life's drama. I loved the smell of my pillow and the deep darkness of night. I loved it because no one needed me there, I could rest. Now my bed mocks me like that athletic kid in gym class knowing dang well I couldn't run the mile in under ten minutes to receive a passing grade. My bed mocks me because it knows how badly I not only want but need sleep. I'm never going to receive a passing grade; I'm not going to get sleep. So, I stand up and start my day. It gets better when I see my girls smile. The sparkles of love in their eyes as they peek up over their crib immediately fill the void that the lack of sleep left on my heart. Then reality sets in as I realize my toddler wet the bed... again, and my infant has poop smeared from toe to ear. "Good morning mommy," they giggle-shout. "Good morning my sweet girls."

Chapter Eleven

I Never Knew

The truth is … I never knew, until today.

As I fumble my way through motherhood, I have come to my knees in thankfulness to my mother. "One day you will realize how amazing your mom is," people would say. In true angsty daughter fashion my response was always, "uh huh". Well, the time has come. I've realized it. Let me set the scene.

My family was hit with the stomach flu. It first started with my oldest, passed to my baby, and landed on me. I don't know how much you know about toddlers, or me for that matter, but for us, stomach bugs mean barf everywhere. It was a flippin' Picasso painting of barf in my home. Floors, clothes, hair, blankets, sheets, toilets, garbage's... barf everywhere. Biohazard zone.

End times were upon us. Death was imminent.

Riding in on her white horse disguised as a truck, my mom came over to help me. I was so sick. I had nothing left. As my mom was holding my baby, I shouted from the other room, "why am I cleaning up sucked-on lucky charm marshmallows off of the floor as the girls laugh at me when I have the flu and have HER barf in MY hair?" My mom smiled at me and calmly explained, "Hannah, because that's motherhood."

That was one of those moments that truly made me a mother. In that moment, I got it. In that moment, every barf, snot drizzle, and poop I had ever ejected outside of the intended landing place flashed through my brain. I laid myself down on the hardwood on top of the soggy cereal that my toddler so lovingly scattered everywhere and felt sorrier than I ever have in my life. Not just an apology and be done with it kind of sorry. But a feel-it-in-my-bones, desire to atone for my sin's kind of sorry. It was in that moment that I realized how much my mom loves me and how much I appreciate and love her unconditionally. I realized all the things she did for me without so much as a thank you. I never knew. I didn't get it, until today. Holy smokes, my mother is a saint. All mothers are saints. I can only hope one day when my girls are older, they will experience this same beautifully crippling realization of my love for them. I also hope they just stop barfing. Just please, stop the barf.

Part Two:

Laugh

"I stood there, pants at ankles, analyzing my next moves. I peek outside the door and see her dancing to music. Now was the time to make a move if ever. I started to squat back on the throne and began to pray. Please don't let her hear me, please don't let her hear me!"

Laughing is my favorite. It is the only thing I ever want to do. Laughing for me is medicine. It cures my soul. When I'm sad, overwhelmed, or down, a good laugh is the only cure I need. Looking at my group of girlfriends, it is no wonder why each one is there. They are hysterical women who share their life stories with an open heart, sprinkled with some laugh-crying and snorting. They are my kind of people.

I belong to a mother's group full of amazing mamas. We are all on different paths and at different places in our journey, but we come together a couple times a month. At our gatherings, we usually have a speaker or activity to help us learn how to cope with the heavy task that is motherhood. I need it! However, I find that what truly helps me in these groups isn't the speaker they thoughtfully chose, or the activities that were specifically designed for us. What helps me the most are the moments before and after the meeting when the other gals and I swap stories of hilarious moments we have endured over the past couple of weeks. The absurd stories make me laugh so hard sometimes I fight for air. The stories let me know that this shit happens to other moms and that I am nowhere near alone. It makes me feel a little relieved to know other moms have crazy children like mine. I love laughing with them because it makes me feel normal.

This part of the book contains some of my hysterical stories laid out in print just for you. In motherhood, there is no need to embellish. I couldn't make this stuff up if I tried! Please feel free to laugh at me, you have my full permission. These things (and much more) happen to all moms on a flipping daily basis and honey there ain't nothing we can do about it!! I want you to be able to learn to laugh. Laugh with other moms and at their stories, laugh with mentors and most importantly learn to laugh at yourself. Once we can do that, I truly believe our souls will be much lighter and brighter. So, without any further ado, laugh-on sister, and please enjoy.

Chapter Twelve

Bad Things

.

The truth is... bad things happen to good people.

I am a strong Christian woman. I follow what I like to think is a strict moral code in which I treat others with respect and love. I try my best to be a good human. I do what I can to help others. I always put my shopping cart in the cart corral. And yet somehow, despite all my good deeds, bad things still happen.

The day I was lambasted in the kneecap with a flippin' frisbee is a day I will never forget. It felt as if I had been shot with a laser gun, I wasn't sure I could continue on with my life. At least not without limb removal surgery. Don't worry, I did continue, barely.

The point is, I'm a good person and bad things sometimes happen to me.

I was at the park with my mom and my two little girls. We walked there after a long day at work because fresh air sounded nice. The park is about a ten-minute walk uphill. I had a double stroller filled with enough snacks to feed half of Texas. After a workout that I don't think I deserved, we arrived. With sweat dripping off my mustache, I pulled my toddler out of the stroller and got ready for the moment. The moment in which she LOVES it and I feel like a good mom. It didn't happen. She wouldn't do the slide, so I forced her by going with her, and we both got slide burns on the back of our legs. It screeched all the way down. "Son of a biscuit I forgot how bad that hurt!"

'Ok' I thought, time to swing! She stone faced me. She straight up looked at me like I was an idiot. 'Ok, not the swing, I get it'. She played for maybe five minutes, fell down in the grass, and went ballistic. Her baby sister followed. Everyone in the park was staring at the ship on fire, that was my life. I loaded my toddler up, got my baby strapped in, and I headed home. At least it's downhill. We got to the other side of the park and things began to cool down. Both girls were quiet, I was walking downhill which made me happy. I survived. I did it. I can do this.

THEN BAM!!!! A lead frisbee straight to the knee!!!! In terms of the actual material of the frisbee, I'm sure it wasn't lead, but it felt like it. "What in the actual fresh cut misery was that?!" I whimpered. Apparently a rogue frisbee escaped its operator. "I'M A GOOD PERSON!!!" I shouted, "I'M DOING MY BEST!"

My toddler giggled, and mom continued talking about something. I can't remember what she was saying, on account of the searing pain. I limped home. As I tuned my mother out due to lack of consciousness, I had a realization.

Bad things happen to good people. Bad things happen to bad people. Heck, bad things happen to all people. It's not a punishment, it's life. Frisbees happen. Hopefully in your case it is not so hard and not to a vital part of the leg. The best we can do is giggle, take a deep breath and limp home, because there is always family waiting to laugh at you once you get there.

Chapter Thirteen

Overdoing It

The truth is... overdoing it is dangerous.

My girls and I were playing upstairs in my room. We were on my bed, which was a dumpster pile of blankets and pillows. My toddler was bringing her babies back and forth between her bedroom and mine as my baby and I tucked them in to go night night. As the number of babies increased and room began to run out, it became funny, to everyone. My girls squealed in excitement to see what would happen if there was no more room.

The last baby doll came by way of blanket burrito tight in my toddler's arms. She was laughing before she even handed me the poor thing. With arms stretched out and with her belly jiggling from gut laughs, her baby made its way into my hands. I looked at my bed, looked at her, then back to the bed. With one swift swoop I swung my arms sideways making room for this new baby and all the others flew through the air. It was a tidal wave of stuffed elephants, dinos, Barbies, babies, and one large octopus. They all hit the wall next to my bed and fell to the ground. Writing a book about motherhood is interesting. Some memories, such as this one, stick out to me. This one is one of my favorites. It was so simple and nothing grand happened, but without spoiling the story, I was forever changed.

My girls fell over with laughter. My baby, who was sitting up, fell completely sideways without even an attempt to catch herself because of the overwhelming power of a hearty gut laugh - it made my heart happy. My toddler dropped to the ground in silence. She was laughing so hard at this point that no sound was coming out anymore. She was wheezing. It was one of the funniest things I have ever seen. I felt like a good mom, finally.

They both laughed for a long time and then composed themselves. My toddler exclaimed, "Oh I LOVE you mama!!" It changed me. That one was genuine. I often prompt my girls with words they can use to express their emotions. But this one, this emotion, was all on her own. She, without prompt, expressed her love for me.

I felt like the coolest mom on the block. It made my ego soar. In my mind, I was the best mom that anyone could have ever hoped to have. I had figured out how to be a good mom. We cleaned up the toys and it was time to make our way downstairs to have a snack after all this fun! I decided then and there they were getting ice cream as a snack today, because I'm such a cool mom today.

As we neared the top of the stairs my eldest turned her body around and laid on her tummy at the top of the stairs' feet down. This is how she slid down our stairs most of the time because it was fun, and it was the fastest. She, still giggling from the stuffed animal catapult moments before, begged me to try it her way. I knew it wouldn't be the most comfortable experience, but who cares, I'm a cool mom now. Let's give it a shot.

I quickly ran my baby down the stairs and placed her at the bottom and then ran with excitement to meet my girl at the top of the stairs. I laid on my belly, feet first, down the stairs and started the slide with my kiddo. Very quickly I realized that I made a mistake. A BIG mistake. The first thing that happened to me was: my boobs, saggy from breast feeding two babies, caught on the first step, momentarily halting my slide. These boobies are no match for my post baby body, so something had to give. In an instant, my sports bra that I wore just about every day flipped up near my chin (along with my tank top) leaving me bare chested on a belly-slide down carpeted stairs.

Loud sounds began to fly from my lips only to be interrupted by the thud of each stair. About halfway down my nipples begin to burn. Well, not burn so much, but felt like the entrance to hell, and I still had another half of a staircase to go. I tried to look down to see if there was anything to do to stop this misery and hit my chin on a stair and bit my tongue. I immediately tasted blood. My knees finally hit the landing and my body stopped.

I swallowed a large gulp of spit and blood and began to assess the damage. Still topless, shirt pressed up to my chin, I looked down. I saw extremely red, raw, carpet burned nipples and belly button. Standing in silence trying to figure out what had just happened to me, I noticed two things. First, I noticed that my toddler was completely oblivious and apparently thought this was a normal occurrence for me. She was already in the kitchen waiting for her snack. Second, I realized while standing there examining and trying to understand this humiliation, I was standing in front of a ground floor, open window. My chest looking like Rudolf and his long-lost twin standing at attention. Completely exposed.

My family and I had just moved into this house a few months before, and I was already going to be labeled the naked lady in the window with weird nipples. Awesome.

I covered my humiliated body and contemplated my life. I chose to slide down the stairs. What was I thinking? Was I so desperate to be the cool mom that I was seriously willing to put my nipples on the line? A memory that is so wonderful for me is overshadowed by hilarious happenstance. Such is the life of a mom.

That night after the girls went to bed, my husband gave me a hug. I flinched, hard. He immediately asked if I was ok. I said yes, and explained I had a back spasm. Now, I never lie to my husband. Ever. I had been so humiliated on the stairs; I couldn't bear to tell him the story. I needed to keep whatever dignity I had left intact. I needed him to not laugh at my bleeding tongue and raw boobs. I needed him to never, under any circumstances, find out. To my knowledge, he never did. Thinking about it now, I probably need to tear these pages out of his copy of the book, so he doesn't feel betrayed. The fact is, my nipples were betrayed that day, and if he's going to ask me to choose between him and my nipples... I choose my nipples.

Although my womanhood will never be the same, I learned something that day. Overdoing it is dangerous.

Upstairs, on my bed with my girls, I felt like a Queen. I felt like a good mom for the first time in a long time. I am so hard on myself; I often find myself worrying about if my girls like having me as a mom. As a perfectionist, I will make sure they do. Trying hard is great but trying too hard is something else entirely. I let the joy of finally feeling like a worthy mother cloud my judgment.

I let it overshadow my common sense.

As parents, we always need to be able to keep our children and ourselves safe, in any circumstance. We need to be protectors in the hard times and the good, without fail. The only sad part of this story is the fact that it took the integrity of my nipples to learn this lesson. So, mama, keep your lady parts inside your bra, have fun with your kids, don't overdo it, and for Heaven sakes, walk down the dang stairs.

Chapter Fourteen

Harder Than It Looks

The truth is.... this is harder than it looks, or maybe not.

Do you have more than one kid in diapers? Because I do. And IT'S HARD.

I don't know about you, but I was never told about how hard it was having two babies close together. I was told about all of the beautiful moments of them growing up together and hitting milestones together. I was told about how happy I would be that they would be so close. Somewhere in this narrative, any talk about logistics had gone out the window. No mention of anything tangible that benefited me. It was all cotton candy ideas and dreams.

I have a two-year-old and an infant, both in diapers. Both are still babies. Both are unapologetically unable to care for themselves. I mean come on; how long can this take?!

My husband often travels for work leaving me home alone with the girls. Usually things go pretty well, including bedtime. Our routine is a life saver, and by 7:00 pm, both girls are sleeping, and mommy gets some time. This is all a reality for NON-bath nights.

Bath nights are different. It's unlike anything I've experienced before, and it's a straight up battle. I love watching both girls giggle in the bubbles, and I am absolutely addicted to the smell of clean babies. It's pure heaven. Sometimes I smell their heads for 15 minutes each after they are in jammies. That reward is more than earned. Getting them from the bath, into jammies, and into bed would be a battle for an octopus mom with eight arms. I have two arms, it's nearly impossible.

I got both girls out of the water onto the rug. As I went to grab the towels, my infant was already on the move. I grabbed her by the ankle as she squealed in delight and slid across the tile floor. My toddler clapped in admiration. I wrapped my oldest in her towel and told her to stay there. I wrapped my smaller potato in the towel just to hear the words, "Mommy, I pottied!" "Mommy on rug!" I left my little wrapped baby burrito on the floor and unwrapped my toddler from her towel. I dunked her in the bathwater, don't judge me, and rewrapped her in the towel.

Clean.

Done.

I went to pick up my baby, and in that time, she had unraveled herself from the towel and was crawling as fast as she could, butt-naked, toward the stairs that weren't gated. Mom-fail, I know.

So, I ran and scooped her up in the nick of time. I went back to the bathroom to find my older daughter hands deep in the toilet. At least it was clean. Whatever. I was beginning to get a little frustrated and winded at this point.

I take both girls into the bedroom and start the lotion slathering process. My girls have such dry skin; this part is undoubtedly a necessity. So, I greased both my pigs and things took a wild and unpredictable turn. My infant had pulled her sister's hair, and all hell was breaking loose in my house. I had no back up. The thought of calling 911 actually went through my mind as this was unfolding but even I thought that was a bit dramatic. I was wrong. I should have called someone, maybe not 911, but someone.

My two greased pigs were now in an all-out diaper-less battle. They were screaming, slapping, hair-pulling, and rolling. I was helpless. I decided my kids need their diapers on ASAP so that was first. Toddler first, let's do this. The problem with that solution is that my toddler had gone into full rigor mortis mode and there was no bending her limbs, especially when they were greased.

Ok, new plan. Infant first, she's more likely to pee anyway. As I grabbed her diaper, she made another run for it, and her tiny slick ankle slipped through my grasp. I crawled after her like a savage. I tackled my baby and wrestled the diaper on her. Once it was on, I closed the door so she could roam free without the fear of her rolling her fat thighs down the flight of stairs.

My toddler was next. She had calmed down a bit, so I began lifting her bottom to place the diaper underneath. At that moment my baby decided once again to slap her sister, straight in the eye. Rigor mortis activated. The baby then pulled her sister's hair. Donkey kick engaged. I blacked out for a bit, but I think I actually shouted, "What in the actual horse's ass is happening right now?! YOU LAY HERE... YOU LAY HERE!!!" I sat on my butt and swung both legs over the girls. One leg per kid. My legs laid over their torsos so as not to crush any air breathing apparatuses. I strapped the final tab of the last diaper on as anger sweat began to pool on my upper lip. I wiped it with the back of my hand and mustered up the strength to not explode.

I find that sometimes that's truly all we can expect of mothers. I stood up and put my baby in her crib with a bottle and sat in the rocker with my toddler. It took about five minutes for everyone to calm down, and for me to stop sweating from pure rage.

I then smelled each girl's head for the allotted fifteen minutes and was glad I was a mom. I wasn't sure how the night ended so well after the toxic battle in which I had just given my all, but it did.

That's motherhood. Those moments right there are what make a mama. Unimaginably hard moments followed by great satisfaction that those beautiful beings are yours. It's weird. It's motherhood. It's so dang funny.

Chapter Fifteen

Sleep Deprivation

The truth is… sleep deprivation is a war tactic.

Up until 2009, the U.S. Military used sleep deprivation as a form of torture/interrogation on its prisoners. It has been used for centuries by many nations as a weapon. Recently, it has been deemed a form of cruel and unusual punishment because it can cause both physical and mental harm. When I say I agree that sleep deprivation is cruel and unusual, I mean it.

I have an infant and a toddler. I haven't slept since 2019. Extreme lack of sleep can cause hallucinations, psychosis, as well as irrational and aggressive actions and language. Honestly, that sounds similar to my attitude most days with these kids. My youngest has decided that sleep is no longer necessary for our family. Big day tomorrow? No sleep for you. Huge workout tomorrow, because this baby weight ain't no joke? No sleep for you. Have the desire to NOT feel like you have been up all night being interrogated by the world's toughest war leader on a bad day? Don't care. No sleep for you.

My first thought when reading about using sleep deprivation during war time was, clearly, they couldn't have been torturing mothers because we've been training for years. Sleep deprivation? Ha. That's called being a mother.

We are asked to do, in my opinion, the most important job one can do: raising our future generation. We are asked to make them polite, honest, kind, not dumb, determined, and the list goes on. We are to help them when they need, feed them when they are hungry, wipe their bums when they are dirty, and make instant decisions that will have lifelong effects. We are asked to do this while withstanding what the U.S. Military said is torture. Seriously? Does this seem ridiculous to anyone else? Honestly, I'm serious. I'm having to do the hardest and most important job I've ever had, while being tortured and interrogated by a toddler. "What is it you want to know, baby girl? All my secrets are yours! Please, for the love of biscuits just GO TO SLEEP!" It gets intense. I'm tired. What's funny is I love being a mother, more than anything. Not funny ha-ha, but funny interesting. I never considered myself a masochist, but ok.

War zones are similar to the home of a mother raising a child. I've never been on the battlefield, but I have chased a naked, poo covered toddler across my parents living room towards the white rug my mother had recently purchased that was literally worth more than my life. When I say I moved with haste to protect my life, I'm not joking. A sound came out of my mouth that I'm not even sure was a distinguishable word, more like the war cries of ancient soldiers ready for battle. Y'all, that's just a typical Tuesday in my house. It's a war zone.

Now please don't take my words literally. My father was a lifer in the Army and has deployed multiple times. My brother was in the Army as well and has also done multiple tours. There was a span of seven years in which every holiday we were missing at least one of them, if not both. I will never make light of being in war or being a soldier. I have never been a soldier, nor do I think I would have the bravery or strength to do so. I will also say that neither of them has been a mother. So, I think mutual understanding is called for. We are all soldiers fighting in a war. Our war zones are just decorated differently. I will also point out that, although sleep deprivation has been outlawed as cruel and unusual for them, it is still a part of my everyday life. With all the respect in my heart, checkmate.

Chapter Sixteen

Working Out

The truth is… I need to start working out.

No one told me that getting your toddler strapped into a car seat would be a cardio event, but here we are. I have never been so jealous or envious of a rodeo ropers tie-down abilities or fitness influencers' stamina. I so yearn for the ability to tie all four of my toddlers' limbs in one slick knot so I could just get her in the car seat. I wish the limited strength of my measly arms could have the stamina to outlast my kid's stiff body. I didn't know that strapping a toddler in a car seat would be straight out of a scene from Kung Fu Panda, arms moving so fast they are no longer appendages, just a blur of motion. Without these skills or strength, the toddler isn't going in. Period.

I vividly remember one beautiful morning in July. It was 89 degrees outside and our garage (where the car is parked) was about 110 degrees. My toddler was already having a morning and it was time to go to my mom's house in hopes that she may raise my children for me that day. I strapped my baby in her side of the car and she cried because it was hot. Fair. I walked around the car to lift my toddler up to her seat, and she wasn't there. Instead of her standing exactly where she was supposed to, which I was expecting for some unknown reason, she was laying on her back in our mud room screaming, "CREAMY!" For those who don't speak toddler, that meant she would like some ice cream. I understood the desire, it was HOT, but I'm not the mom to give my girls ice cream at 8am. My answer was no kid, get in the car. I resorted to "helping" her get in the car. I lifted her limp body off the mud room floor and immediately began to sweat, from anger or heat, I wasn't sure. As I made my way to the car door, I turned to make sure the mud room door shut, and in the process smacked my kid's head on the work bench. Shit. In my head, I was thinking how maybe she got what was coming… maybe? No? Ugh, I'm a monster. So, I heaped her up closer to my chest and hugged her tight. I asked to see the ouchie and to my delight, no blood, bump, or even scratch. Thank God. By this time, my infant had completely lost her marbles (I'm sure due to the heat), and the butt crack of my leggings were now starting to show the efforts of my labor. I opened the car door to the opera that was my infant and started strapping my large kid in.

Anyone ever play 'Light as a feather, stiff as a board as a kid? Just curious. Her body got so ridged she would give a coroner a run for his or her money. She wasn't budging. She would not sit without CREAMY! When I say that I'm not proud of my actions, I mean it. I karate chopped her in the waistline in hopes that it would make her bend… fill in judgement here… I know. It didn't work. Sweat had now started to pool on my upper lip, and I was so angry I needed a break. Plus, my kid had twisted her way around so that her front side was facing the car seat. That wasn't going to work. All the while, my infant was still screaming to the Heavens. I backed away in defeat to come up with a different strategy. I physically wiped my brow and walked out of the garage to catch my breath. As I placed my hands on my hips and looked up to Heaven, I saw someone out of the corner of my eye. I had to laugh, and I wish I could describe the looks on the neighbor kids' faces, but I'm not that talented of a writer. The closest I can get is a combination of horror, fear, and confusion. They quietly asked, "Is she ok?" I responded, "Yes, she's not hurt." Which is technically a lie because of the work bench situation. They actually took a step backwards and went inside their house. I audibly laughed. It was what I needed. I approached my mini and held her in my arms. I walked around the car and grabbed my infant's car seat and removed her from the heat. We all sat on the grass for about three minutes catching our breath. We then got in the car, everyone buckled, and went to my mom's.

Some days are harder than others. As moms, we know the ups and downs and in-betweens of raising children. They have off days and so do we, and that's okay. That is completely normal. I don't recommend using any sort of karate move on children but if you ever have, you're not alone. We are not only moms, but we are also human. We do the very best we can, given our current circumstances. This day was not my best day. I'll do better the next time. However, I wish I would maintain a workout routine to give me a leg up on my kiddos (or at least to minimize the perspiration) on days like that.

Chapter Seventeen

Real Life

The truth is... I'm not even sure this is real life anymore.

This is what has happened in my life over the past week:

1. I've been thrown up on over 20 times. (Yes, I counted because I was genuinely curious how much my projectile spewing infant was actually capable of.)

2. Cleaned up Cheez-It's that have been river danced on because I left my toddler alone for less than one minute while I peed. Was it my fault? Yes, yes it was.

3. Gotten play slapped on the face.

4. Got human feces under my fingernails.

5. Smelled the vicious stench of a week's worth of rotting diapers because I let the diaper genie bag bubble open. I. Almost. Died.

6. Choked on a cheerio. Me, I did.

7. Slipped on vomit in my kitchen, throwing me into a whole-body-fear spasm and straining my groin.

8. Said curse words that no Christian mother should ever say, let alone in front of her children while doing a whole-body-fear spasm

induced by vomit.

9. Apologized to my kids for being wrong.

10. Blasted the ever-loving glory out of my shin bone on my glider chair's footstool.

Motherhood is not for the faint of heart. It is not for the weak or proud. It takes the woman we used to be and makes her into this incredible being that can use love to overcome all. Although all of these things truly and actually happened to me this week, so did the following.

1. My baby girl cried for her mama and when I held her, she stopped. That was pretty cool.

2. My kid held out her hand and shouted, "come on mama!!!" Because she was excited to experience the park WITH me. That felt the best.

3. My toddler nuzzled deep into my neck, sniffed, and could barely yell "so stinky!!!" before she full blown belly laughed. I laughed so hard, and I needed it.

4. I watched my infant sleep, and there is truly nothing more peaceful or sweeter.

5. My two-year-old sassy pants couldn't wait to show me her "art project" from preschool. It was confusing and unidentifiable, but I loved it, especially after she told me it was a coloring of me. We'll work on it, ha-ha.

6. Watching Papa, my dad, tell my toddler to "get your butt over here" in his funny yet gruff voice, and watching her stick her booty out and walk backwards to him giggling.

7. Was called "Mama" countless times over the span of a week. It feels good. Every. Single. Time.

8. My infant laugh-squeal screamed when she saw me walk through the door and clapped her hands in approval. It's nice to be wanted.

9. Watched my two girls build their friendship and sisterly bond. My oldest held the younger in her arms and kissed her.

10. Realized how incredibly blessed I am with my two littles.

Sure, the first list happened. But so did the second. Being a mom means all of these things and a million more happen all at once, continuously, until you die. Sorry my friend, you're in it for the long haul. I'm just here as a humble servant to tell you the truth. I want you to know the things that no one told me. If you're already a mom, I'm sure you already know this, so I hope you then can find a friend in my words. I hope you can find hope and comfort in knowing that other moms are going through this too. I hold up some sort of hand signal into the air with solidarity in my heart. I see you. We can choose to look at the first list as hard, negative, and daunting. We can also choose to laugh hard at it, because the good Lord knows how funny it truly is.

Chapter Eighteen

Poop

The truth is... she had to poop.

About a week ago, my husband, my daughter, and I all decided it was time for her to transition into her big girl bed. It was an awesome day. Well, in full disclosure it was actually an awful day filled with bickering between my husband and I. We are best friends, so arguing rarely happens, but that day, it did. After blood, sweat, and tears were put into the building of her new bed and dresser, it turned out amazing. It was so cute. She got to pick all the colors, which didn't match or have any design scheme of course, but she was so proud. As most mothers know, the transition isn't always easy. I knew to prepare myself for the trouble to come. My husband and I rekindled our love over a cold can of beer after the girls went to sleep and laughed about the day and all of its struggles. He truly does make me happy and has his very own way of driving me absolutely bonkers.

A few nights passed with my big girl in her own bed. She did really good. She needed help falling asleep the first night, but that's about it. Nighttime sleep comes easy for my oldest and I am so thankful. Napping, however, is a different story entirely. She always napped well in her crib, but somehow moving to a big girl bed created an unwritten agreement that naps were no longer part of the deal. She gets up and plays, cries, rolls around in her blankets until she resembles a suffocating tamale - she does it all.

About a week into this transition, with funny things happening every day at nap, she did the Granddaddy of them all. I kind of secretly looked forward to nap time every day that week just to see what kind of tricky things she was going to do, but nothing could have prepared me for this particular day.

I was downstairs working on a website launch for my boutique, when I heard her door open. I waited in silence to see what the move was. I heard nothing. Fear began to well in my heart that she may have made a move towards her sleeping sister's door, so I yelled up the stairs, "Go lay down in your big girl bed! It's nap time!" She appeared on the top of the stairs and made direct eye contact with me. She had rolled one too many times in her bed because her shirt was completely twisted and both pigtail rubber bands were long gone, leaving fan shaped hair sticking out both sides of her head. With all the drama she could muster in her tiny little body, she held both hands in front of her, palms up. She shook them at me and yelled, "HANNAH, I HAVE TO POOP!!!! UGHHH" This. How do I possibly not burst into laughter?! This moment right here is not only funny, but where everything we have learned about mothering is put to the test. I know that ANY reaction to a toddler is affirmation of her behavior, so a laugh would only tell her I was enjoying it. I couldn't have that. I needed her to learn to not get out of bed, I needed her to learn to not call me by my first name. I needed to step away and not pee my pants in laughter!!

We have been teaching her our first names so if she is ever lost, she can tell someone our name and not just mom or dad. Learning this gave her a strange source of power.

She has since been using our names in correct context, and it is hysterical.

I gently asked her, "You need to poop?" Only a small snort from the pent-up laughter came out when I asked her. She responded, "yes". As I grabbed her hand and walked with her to the potty, I had to physically put a hand over my mouth to control my laughter. As she sat and did her job on the toilet, we of course had the conversation that my name is Hannah, but you call me, "Mommy." End of story. In our house, it's a respect issue.

We were both sitting in silence waiting for the job to be done. She filled the silence with the following, "big girls poop lots, Mommy." I laugh hard and loud. I couldn't help it. It came from my gut. So, I woke up my other sleeping daughter from her nap, ruined nap time for both kids, and didn't get to have one spare minute to myself that day.

Ya know, you win some and lose some.

The truth is, that's ok with me.

I find the experiences that most make a mother are the times when we can see the beauty in the crap. Sometimes quite literally. Step back, mama, and realize that this happens to every mom. You are not alone, and you are one heck of a good mom.

Chapter Nineteen

Black Eye

The truth is... Jesus gave me a black eye.

I was in this adorable little bookshop in the mountains and found this incredible picture Bible for my daughters. I debated getting it because I was pretty sure it weighed way too much for either one of them to lift. I thought to myself that I would be reading it to them anyway so, no bother. I was so excited to read it to them. I loved when my mother shared the Bible with me as a young girl, and I couldn't wait to pass on the tradition. It was going to be so special.

Later that night, just before bedtime, I surprised the girls with the book. They giggled uncontrollably at the mere size of the thing and my toddler proclaimed she was a "BIG GIRL" as she lifted it with both hands (and her entire body). It was one of those moments that rarely happen in the life of a mother. Both my kids smelled incredible from the bath their dad had just given them. They were both fed healthy dinners and had clean pajamas on their bodies. I was clean, relatively, and comfortable in my favorite sweatshirt. It was perfect. I think the carpet was recently vacuumed as well, which never happens in my house. I called both girls to sit on my lap, and we opened the book. I was always under the impression that opening the Bible would release a piece of Heaven, but in my experience that night, it wasn't true. As soon as I opened this beautiful book full of hope, redemption, and peace, my infant ripped the page directly in half.

Unfixable. Broken.

I love books more than I love most things, so the damage was devastating. I thought to myself, "Calm down, deep breaths, no matter, let's continue". As soon as my infant ripped the page, it was like all bets were off. My toddler started to slap the book, pull the pages, scream in laughter, and throw her body directly back at me with joy. Now as a mom, I was actually kind of impressed that my kids had such love for the Bible. Had I done it? Had I raised God following women already? Yeah? Oh, boy. Nope. I didn't. Not yet at least.

What was fun and exciting soon turned into a violent power struggle between my girls - who was allowed to hold the pages of the book and who was not. My toddler, God love her, was going to win. Now, this would have been fine if my infant didn't have the vice grip that rivaled that of modern machinery.

As my baby held the pages of Luke with a cement hand, my toddler lifted the book up and away with all of her might (which is a surprising amount). My baby finally let go of this giant Bible that weighed more than a legitimate bowling ball, and if flew up and made contact with my cheek and eye. The words that then flew from my mouth were neither Christian, nor appropriate. I believe I disappointed Jesus that evening. I was trying so hard to do a good thing, and I ended up with an all-out brawl. As tears poured down both mine and my toddler's face, my infant giggled. My husband came upstairs, and without asking any questions, he grabbed both kids and went downstairs. I sat in silent sobs trying to figure out if I was permanently blind on top of my presumed biblical concussion. Why did this happen? Why would Jesus give me a black eye?

Here's the question I should have asked myself. When things go wrong, why do I always blame God first? I know full well that Jesus didn't actually give me a black eye, but sitting there in my pain and sadness, I felt victimized. I was doing a good thing and look what happened. I wanted to give up, but then I had a thought. Did Satan just win? Just the mere thought of that made something deep within me so mad that my body temperature actually rose. When I say I'm competitive, it's an understatement. It was an "aww hell naw" moment. If I was wearing hoop earrings, I would have pulled them out, ready to fight.

I pulled myself to my feet, wiped away my snot, and pulled it together. I marched downstairs with this 14-pound weapon and declared I would see, "victory tonight!" Yes, I said that. Although my husband was a bit frightened, he helped me buckle both girls into their table chairs. I read some of my favorite parts of the Bible to my girls from across the table. They were also four feet apart and strapped down, so it went much better. Mom won that night. Jesus won. When Jesus and mama win in the same night, it's cause for celebration, my friend.

After the girls went to bed, I sat with pure satisfaction knowing that in the future, somehow, the story of Jesus giving me a black eye would be a vehicle to inspire others. And here we are. You're welcome.

When small moments seem to defeat you, I encourage you to get competitive. Let Jesus win. Stand up, come up with a plan, even if it's on the fly, and fight for your family. Make love win. Make your family win. Make Jesus win and forget the rest. You may find yourself hurt or with a black eye, but that is a small price to pay for the victory of your family, I promise.

Chapter Twenty

Leavenworth

The truth is... they should put toddlers in Leavenworth.

I have a weird obsession with prison shows.

Yea, I know, let it go.

I got to thinking. How can the prison systems in real life reduce the chance of returning inmates? Toddlers. Hear me out.

Today I was cleaning my bedroom. Laundry was put away, baby changing station organized, and shoes put in the closet. Sweat rolled down my unwashed face as I finally finished. I did it, I put away the one million items my family has left around the house. I am not sure how this became the mom's job, but it did. It is some weird unwritten rule that I am the official picker-upper of random items. On the rare occurrence that this task gets completed, I am proud. I am proud of my ability to multitask and exercise and clean and cry and feel encouraged and sing all at the same time. It's a sight to see, really.

Can I get an "Amen!"?

I wiped my brow and turned around. The site I saw was crippling. My charismatic toddler decided to help me rearrange... everything. The shoes were in the diaper station, the diapers were lined up in a quite impressive line, the books were on the chair, and the folded laundry... not. so. folded. It was my fault really; I turned my back for 30 seconds. Lesson learned, again.

In that moment, I longed to be out amongst the world, with adults, with anyone really. I wanted to be anywhere but the natural disaster that was currently my life.

So, back to my thought. Make crying robot toddlers to put in each prison cell and require of the inmates a quiet, clean, and safe environment. It's an impossible task. They will work their hardest to complete the mission that is doomed to fail from the beginning. Those prisoners will NEVER want to return! Toddlers are the answer.

Now please don't mistake me, I love my kids. However, sometimes raising them feels like cruel and unusual punishment. As a mother, I often find myself on the brink of insanity, asking God what lesson He is trying to teach me that day. If I have to ask my toddler not to throw snacks at the dog one more time, I'm going to lose it. If we forced inmates to endure this type of cruel and unusual punishment, maybe they wouldn't reoffend for fear that they would have to return to their toddler-destroyed cell and back to the reality that so many mothers face on a daily basis. So next time ol' Slick Rick is asked to steal a car, I bet his answer would be, "sorry I'm busy. I will never go back to that cell; I'm not cut out to be a mother." Me either Slick Rick, me either. Robot toddlers in prison cells, follow me for more life hacks.

Chapter Twenty-One

I Wanted to Poop

The truth is... I just wanted to poop.

I have been working on potty training my toddler. As many of you know, it's all about consistency and routine. For example, our routine is to pull pants down, poop, paper, flush, pants up, wash, dry, done. Over and over. Day after day. I must begin this story by saying that everyone poops and pees. Yes, even moms.

One day, just like any other, I had to use the bathroom. My daughter was playing fairy dress up, so she was wearing a tutu skirt, a wicker bonnet, and holding a star wand that had long strings hanging from it. She was elated at the majesty of her own presence. As I walked towards the bathroom, I noticed she was following me and asking with great hope, "Poop? Poop mama?" I half laughed and said "Yes, I have to poop on the potty just like you."

As soon as we both enter our spare bathroom, she shouts, "pants down!" and slaps my butt with her wand. It's a half bath, and I tell you this so you can better visualize the space and what is happening. I giggle and follow the command. After I barely contacted the ice-cold porcelain, my fairy-clad daughter shouted, "POOP MAMA!" Now, as a mom with absolutely no shame left, I will tell you that yes, I indeed pooped. It was not as fast as my toddler would have liked, because I was asked no fewer than 24 times if I was "all done". I don't know how many of you have pooped under pressure like this, but let me tell you, it's not as easy as it sounds.

After I got one out that relieved the pressure, I decided to give up and announce, "All done". She then slaps the paper roll with her wand and declares, "PAPER". At this point, I am scared. Her demands are fast, loud, and to the point, as if she was running a country and there was a punishment waiting if I did not abide. As I quickly wiped my butt, my two-year-old made sure that I knew to "WIPE GOOD, MOMMY!!" When I stood up and reached for my pants, I realized that a true tragedy was about to happen. My toddler forgot some steps. She pointed her wand in the direction of the sink and demanded that I, "WASH HANDS". I was going to ask about my pants, but before I got a sound out, she demanded once again, "WASH HANDS MOMMY".

Pants down, pride long gone, I waddle to the sink and wash my hands. "Good job, Mommy," she says with a wand slap on the booty, and then takes her leave.

She left me there with my pants around my ankles, my pride hurt, and my brain very confused as to what the hell had just happened. Apparently, my kid thinks she's the Shit Fairy, or the ruler of a country, I wasn't sure. I've truly created a monster.

As I mentioned before, I wiped very quickly out of pure fear. I wasn't sure the job was done to my satisfaction, but I was scared to re-wipe because of the consequences from the defecation fairy. I stood there, pants at ankles, analyzing my next moves. I peek outside the door and see her dancing to music. Now was the time to make a move if ever. I started to squat back on the throne and began to pray. Please don't let her hear me, please don't let her hear me! The fear that pulsated through my veins as I tried to complete this secret butt wipe mission was palpable in the air. As soon as I thought I was in the clear, who appeared but this fairy dictator. She looked so excited as she asked, "GO AGAIN MOMMY? MORE POOP?" I didn't know how to explain to my toddler that even though she asked if I wiped good, I didn't. I truly didn't know how to explain that, like seriously. So, I said yes, more poop. She demanded again the routine, this time remembering pants. Thank heavens. As I finished washing my hands, she stayed in the bathroom this time, and followed me out. She wanted to make sure the job was finished. With my head hung in disgrace, and with curiosity about what would happen after I left the bathroom, I took my seat at our kitchen table next to my much-deserved Diet Coke.

At first, I thought, "WHAT JUST HAPPENED?? CAN I NOT EVEN GO POOP IN MY OWN HOME?!?!"

Then I began to laugh a little. She was just following the routine and wanted to see me succeed. Then came the deeper thoughts: I wonder if this is how she feels? I wonder if, in the mundane routine of it all during potty training, my tone became demanding towards her? I wonder if I bark orders like she did to me and if it makes her feel how I felt - confused, exhausted, and a little bit confused to be honest. Even though my job got finished, it felt rushed and I kind of still felt like I had to go some more. Did I do that to her? Did I rush her job and confuse her with quick instructions?

Why as moms do we see life as an endless to-do list that we feel like we need to complete as efficiently as possible? Why is it so hard to slow down and let my daughter get all of her poop out of her butt before we move on to the next activity? Why am I in such a damn rush, honestly? Toddlers and their potty schedules can truly teach you a lot about your own patience and endurance. It can slow us down, make us wait, and show us that slow moments in life are not really that bad - especially when done in a rainbow tutu.

Chapter Twenty-Two

Kids Flip

The truth is… apparently kids flip.

Some days I'm a good mom, some days I daydream about my kids being on a rocket ship to the moon. You know, balance. I often take these daydreams for a ride. In this particular dream, I acknowledge that renting a rocket ship would be completely unreasonable, too expensive of course. So, I think of alternative ways of how I could get my kids to the moon, economically. I followed this thought to one of those large blow-up contraptions that one person sits on one end and another person jumps on the other end, thus catapulting the first person unreasonably high in the air. What if I put my kids in their Bumbo chairs on one of those blow-up things and I then jumped… would they reach the moon? Probably not, also not the safest option. I'll reassess it later.

I was doing my daily task of laundry. Laundry in my house never seems to cease. No matter how many loads I do, or how quickly I get them done, I am always putting more dirty clothes in the dang hamper. It's dark magic and I don't appreciate it. I rebuke laundry, in Jesus' name. So anyway, I was doing the laundry and I decided to let my little watch TV while I did. I know, she's going to grow up into a psychopath, I'm sure. So, I plopped her in her Bumbo chair probably too close to the edge of my bed, because I needed the space for laundry, and I turned on the tube.

I worked endlessly. I put socks in pairs and folded pants. I hung up shirts and put the undies away in drawers. My girl just sat and watched. She was so peaceful that I didn't want to move her in any way. I was honestly scared to make eye contact in fear of ending this blissful and extremely rare moment. If you know, you know.

I finished my laundry, and everything was cleaned up and put away. I decided I needed a rest. With all my weight, I threw myself backwards onto my bed. At the very moment I should have been feeling a huge sigh of relief, I caught movement out of the corner of my eye. I turned my head just in time to see my baby, still sitting in her Bumbo, completely upside-down and whirling through the air towards the floor. The shriek that came from my mouth, ladies and gentlemen, rivaled that of a dying cat. I have never gotten out of bed so quickly. My feet just hit the floor when I heard the thud. I ran as fast as I could to my baby. I was sure one of four things was going to be true. One, she was dead. Two, every limb was going to be detached from her body. Three, she was dead. And four, she was surely dead. As I rounded the corner of my bed, there sat my baby, upright, still in her Bumbo. I had never been so thankful for her big fat thighs. They kept her in the chair. She had landed her very first complete front flip, flawlessly. I was kind of impressed. I held my girl and cried. I was so ashamed of myself. My girl was perfectly fine, but I wasn't.

Apparently, kids can do front flips. Who knew? I learned something that afternoon: There are reasons that toys have rules and regulations. We should probably follow them. I am sure that placing my kiddo in a Bumbo on a soft surface three feet off the ground near the edge was against some kind of rule. I used to always say, "Oh, it's fine. Nothing will happen when I'm watching." Girl, get out of that mindset. Although I have a funny story to laugh at now, that could have gone deadly wrong.

So, if you were also daydreaming like me, and wondering how to get your child to the moon - although they do fly off the edge of the bed if you flop on the other side, they do not in fact reach the moon. Maybe paying for a rocket ship isn't so bad after all. Maybe there are safety belts and childcare?

Part Three:
Grow

"We are tired, I'm with you. I strive each day to make more moments funny instead of angry. After time I began to see funny moments outweigh the angry ones, and that's all I can hope for. Progress over perfection."

To say I have grown as a woman since becoming a mom may be the greatest understatement of the century. I am a completely different person than who I was pre-children. I am guessing you are too. There is so much to learn when becoming a mother, and so much is asked of us from the very second we give birth to our children. It's kind of unfair really, at least I think so. We need to learn how to care for this new human, how to feed it, how to bathe it, how to take care of that gross scab on its weird belly button. We need to learn how to stay true to who we are, while changing entirely. We need to continue to learn to be a good wife, when all the while a joy sucker is hanging off of our nipple. It's a lot. I believe that we need to learn all of this to be good mamas, and with haste.

I have also learned that we don't need to reinvent the wheel. Moms have gone before us for centuries and will continue to come after us. Things have been done well, and not so well, and we can learn from all of it. As a mom, I still have so much to learn, but I have a lifetime to learn it. With the help of those around me, I know I can.

This section of the book shows you the tips, tricks and lessons I have learned along the way. I have made some huge mistakes, not only as a mother, but as a wife and as a woman, and I want to share it with you so you can avoid those same mistakes if at all possible. I have also come to some pretty awesome thoughts about life that I think would be a travesty to keep to myself. I wouldn't be doing my job as a member of the mom club if I remained silent. The following section is not a law book or rules to follow, just mere observations and lessons I've learned. I must reiterate, I am not an expert, a medical professional or a licensed counselor. I am a mom. Plain and simple. I am a mom who is walking the same path as you. Take it for what it's worth. Take it with a grain of salt and take it with love. After all, with love is how I hope to deliver it. Let's dive in.

Chapter Twenty-Three

Someone Died

The truth is… someone died.

There were so many moments after I had my first baby that shocked me. There were a whole host of new emotions and challenges. There were new joys and tasks. The thing that shocked me the most about this new and wonderful transition into motherhood was this crippling sadness deep within me. I know postpartum depression effects many women, including myself, but this wasn't that. It was different.

The first few weeks as a mom are crazy. Our days are filled with diapers and bottles, crying and laughing. New transitions and hard lessons. Sleep deprivation and snuggle sessions. The first few weeks are full of new adventures, so it's a bit more expected that they'll be tough to get through.

But as the weeks went on, I watched as everyone's lives went back to normal. Everyone went back to work, and back to their normal lives, except for me. The whole world got back to normal, except for me. I was still right here going through the challenges alone, because my husband and help mate had returned to the real world. I was stuck at home with this beautiful screaming baby in a body I no longer recognized.

Everything about me was different. Especially my thoughts. The depth of who I was changed the minute I had a baby, and I can't quite put into words what that tangible thing was that changed, but it did. My wants and needs were different. My likes and dislikes were different. My body was different and still betraying me with excess bleeding and bloating, stitches and scars. I was so lost. I felt as if I had been transported into someone else's life that I didn't recognize or want, and I was expected to not only stay there, but thrive.

As a month or two passed, I still had this deep sadness in my heart. It felt like I missed something or someone, but I didn't know who or what. I didn't even know where to begin looking. My focus in those times was to get through each day with all parties still breathing at the end. That was it, that's all I could do.

I was out on a walk with my baby girl one fall evening and thoughts of who I used to be flooded my mind. Thoughts of funny moments with friends and of my husband and I enjoying a date night filled with way too many Moscow Mules. I thought of fun trips and all the books I still wanted to read. Those poor books now sat in a pile I knew dang well wouldn't be touched for years. I thought of trips to the grocery store by myself and being able to drive my car in peace without having to drown out the cries with music, but rather cranking that jam up with the window down and letting the warm wind blow my hair into another dimension. My thoughts came back to the present and I noticed tears had been streaming down my face. It was an uncontrollable and unrecognized emotion. I was lonesome, but I was surrounded by support. I was sad, but absolutely loved my newborn. What was this intense thing bubbling up inside me?

All at once I realized it. I missed someone. I missed me. I was no longer the woman I used to be (and that's the absolute truth). I also knew that no matter how hard I tried, she was never going to come back. Sure, certain things about who I am will eventually come back over time, but who I was as a whole will never return. After realizing this in its complexity, I had to stop pushing the stroller, put my hands on my knees and wail in sorrow. I cried hard, loud, and uncontrollably. It felt really good. I missed me. I wanted me back.

I will say that I love the woman I am becoming as a mother. She is way more awesome than who I used to be. But in that moment on the sidewalk, I let it out. I was so incredibly sad, and I needed release.

Just then, a car drove up and stopped next to me. This middle-aged man yelled out, "You alright?" His words scared the tarnation straight out of me as I had not noticed the car had stopped over my sobbing. I jumped about three feet in the air and whipped my head around, snot flinging everywhere. I was ugly crying to its fullest. I wiped the snot, hair, and tears and replied, "what?" He repeated his question, and I heard him put his car in park. I explained, "I just had a baby and it's a hard transition. I just needed to cry. I'm sorry I scared you. I'm ok." He stared at me in silence for a bit. I assured him I was fine, and he drove off slowly staring at me through the rear view.

I began to laugh uncontrollably. That poor man. He was just having a normal evening until my hurricane of a mess crossed his path. He probably contemplated calling the police because a crazy lady with a baby was having a complete melt down. I wouldn't have blamed him one bit!

I had finally started to understand this sadness that lurked in my soul. I was mourning the loss of myself. I was grieving me. Once I realized what this was and had my complete meltdown, I was able to move forward.

I was able to see that the best is yet to come. Hell yeah, the woman I used to be was amazing. She was strong, independent, and sassy. She was fit and funny and goal driven. What was now left of me was a confused, lonely woman who smelled like barf. It was quite the difference. I knew deep down that once I survived this thing called motherhood, I was going to be even stronger. Even funnier. I was going to thrive (once I stopped crying of course).

When a woman becomes a mother, her old self must die. We become warriors. We become this incredible new version of ourselves that can overcome any challenge because of the love that is instantly in our heart the moment that fat potato comes out of our body. We become new. We become absolutely awesome. There is a distinct difference between who we were before that moment and who we are after. The old us dies and the new warrior emerges, just like a phoenix from the ashes. So, although we do need to mourn the loss of our old selves, I also believe we should celebrate the woman we are becoming. We need to be praised by those around us for the incredible things we are doing, but most of all, we need to be praised by our own selves. We need to recognize these changes in ourselves and be proud! It's sad, yes. But it is all together wonderful in the exact same moment. Cry it out mama, because the best version of you is still growing. And she will shock the heck out of you, if you let her.

Chapter Twenty-Four

Progress Over Perfection

The truth is... progress is better than perfection.

Today my toddler vaselined my infant. You may not have realized that "vaselined" was an actual word, but now you know. Was she trying to mimic mommy putting on her lip gloss? Probably. Was she trying to slick her down so we might just slide through the gate of Heaven? Possibly. Now, it wasn't quite so bad as the pictures you see online with the baby covered from head to toe in jelly, but it was enough to make me question where I went wrong as a mother. How did I let this happen? I was simply trying to change the bedding, so my husband and I didn't have to sleep in the spit up that my darling girl left for us the night before. As I wiped the goo from my little one's eyebrow, I began to laugh. You just can't make this up. I laughed hard, and for a long time. Motherhood happens in moments. It happens in moments like these where things go wildly unexpectedly and hilariously off track. I've learned that down here in the trenches of being a mommy, we must learn to laugh. We need to let go of control because it's what drives our anger. If we are somehow able to step back from these frustrating situations and see them as the hysterically funny oddities that they are, life as a mom becomes a little easier.

Moments happen over and over like a relentless and forceful ocean wave. Just like the ocean, the wave can be both fiercely unforgiving and beautifully serene in the exact same moment - it just depends on how you're looking at it. The hard times of motherhood won't ever stop. I know, that's depressing. Even the hard moments, when looked at through the lenses of love, grace, and a little bit of humor can be moments of hope and laughter instead of struggle and defeat. They can be ways for us to connect with our children through learning, failing, and getting back up. Our kids will see us struggle. We spend so much time with them that it's inevitable. It's what we do with these moments that matters. While your children are watching are you going to lie down and accept defeat with an angry heart and harsh words, or are you going to step back, laugh a little, and overcome the challenge with grace? That, my beautiful mama friend, is completely up to you. What will your moments look like?

I must add that just like you, the above words are great in theory but almost impossible to implement as a struggling mom. We are tired, I'm with you. I strive each day to make more moments funny instead of angry. After time I began to see funny moments outweigh the angry ones, and that's all I can hope for. Progress over perfection.

Chapter Twenty-Five

Mistakes

The truth is.... I make mistakes.

So, in the past month or so...

1. My daughter fell off my bed.

2. I fell asleep for the night without turning the monitor on... and woke up in a panic thinking she was in need, and I was in dreamland.

3. I yelled at my husband over an Instant Pot button... honestly, I did that. Then promptly apologized.

4. My kids watched more TV this week than I will publicly admit... because you know... I'm tired. Their brains are now fried. I know it. Please say a prayer for my future psychopaths.

5. My kid pulled my cleaning rag out of the laundry and sucked on it... effects yet to be determined. Oh, my sweet little lab rat.

6. I didn't catch my toddler at the end of the slide because I thought she had it... she didn't. She shot so far, I had to actually walk to her, and her beanie was knocked off her head. After helping her get the woods chips out of her mouth and ears, she seemed to bounce back quickly... pun intended.

7. I underestimated the size of my backside and effectively

booty bounced my kid into the refrigerator... the door was open... she went IN the fridge.

8. I thought I was a bad mom, more than once.

Do you know how hard it is to keep a toddler alive?! It's hard. I'm a heck of a mama, and you know why? It's not because I do everything perfectly... because, uh, read the list again. It's because I care about all the above. Mommin' has a learning curve. You bet I learned something from every single experience above. I learned how to better protect and care for my child, my marriage, and myself. I learned that mistakes happen, and it's ok.

Ok perfectionists like me, let me repeat that.

Mistakes happen, and it's ok.

Also, if you're anything like me, you hate it when those mistakes are in front of others.

As a mom who is still figuring things out, I can say with certainty there is something so special and forgiving to my soul when I see other moms having a hard time... I know I'm a monster. It's not that I want anyone to struggle, I truly don't. I just need to be reminded that I'm not alone. This stuff is hard. Kids are chaos. Wonderful, but chaos. We are all doing our best, and to see another mama in exactly the same place I am is encouraging. I often want to give moms around me in the community high fives because our kids are still alive... and that's amazing. Because of the Covid pandemic and its effect on mothers everywhere, I just hold up the Mocking Jay symbol and whistle letting them know I would volunteer as tribute for them if I could.

My daughters are still amongst the living world, praise God. Being a mom is the hardest, most unforgiving thing I've ever attempted. Mistakes happen, and it's ok. Finally, snacks, if they aren't bleach filled cleaning rags, fix most all situations for both mama and littles. Mom on.

Chapter Twenty-Six

Prayer

The truth is… prayers get silly when you're a mom.

Prayer. The quiet time with God. Our time to just be us and ask for what we desperately and truly think we need. No need to hide anything when praying, my friend, because the good Lord already knows what's on your heart. He knows what we need and when we need it. He knows what we hide, even from ourselves.

Prayers get funny when you're a mom. If I pray one more time for that lost chicken nugget my kid found and ate to not have some sort of rare food disease, I think God is going to strike me with lightning. I joke, He wouldn't do that… yet. Over the years, I have heard some of the funniest prayers from mamas.

"Please God, let my kid sleep for like 30 min during nap so I can just finish that last episode of Yellowstone."

"Please Lord, help me find my car key that my daughter hid so my husband doesn't lose his marbles…again."

"Please God, make my house spotless without me having to lift a finger."

"Lord, if you could prevent my kid from going bonkers in Target today, that'd be great. Thanks."

"God, if you could make Jack not die in the Titanic today that would be super. I can't possibly handle another emotional meltdown this morning."

I have heard it all. I'm here to tell you that God doesn't mind one bit, He enjoys hearing your prayers, no matter how silly.

I often wonder if God designed it this way to get a good laugh. I bet He knew all along that women get to this point in motherhood where our requests are utterly ridiculous. I mean, it's got to be hysterical to listen to a mother, covered in vomit, ask for one, JUST ONE DAY, where her clothes are free of bodily fluids... that aren't her own. It has to bring a chuckle when a worn-out mother begs for the cheerio lodged in her son's ear to find its way out on its own without a doctor's visit. If I was listening to it all, I know I'd laugh. There are many times in this journey where I've straight asked Jesus if he was pranking me.

I think it's healthy to vent to our Father. I think He alone is the only person who knows our truest story and He alone is the one that can see the bigger picture. I find that telling someone my deepest fears, struggles, triumphs, or secrets really creates a bond between us. Trusting someone with that personal information about ourselves can be extremely stressful. Will she tell other moms? Can she relate to me, or am I in fact actually crazy? Will she laugh at me behind my back? All these things go through my mind. Sometimes I can't bring myself to tell other people things because it's too deep or too scary. Those are the things I leave for God. Those are the moments when I trust no one else with my dirty laundry, and in those moments, Jesus and I really grow together.

I know prayers get silly and can be a funny topic, but they can also save your life. Just like so many other topics, in motherhood the spectrum is large. It can range from laughing through a prayer telling God all about how your kid penguin slid down the stairs, to crying out in pure isolation because no one can truly understand what you're going through. I get it. I've personally experienced both. Here's a secret: both prayers are beautiful and normal. Both prayers are a way to connect to the one who made us. He and only He can give us comfort during this crazy ride of being a mom. Stay prayed up girl.

Chapter Twenty-Seven

What We Say

The truth is… we really need to be careful what we say to people.

I was out shopping with my girls the other day. I had my diaper bag on my back, a kid in each arm, and the weight of the world's disappointment on my shoulders. It showed all over my face, I'm sure. As I was trying to tune out the piercing sounds of my toddler crying because she couldn't have more ice cream, I looked over to see a woman smiling at me. She said to me, "cuties!" I responded with, "Thank you! They are cute, but man do they keep me busy!" I was trying to be authentic and maybe hint at the fact that, at this point I may have wanted to sell my children for a can of peas. Unfortunately, the woman didn't catch on. She laughed and said, "Oh you just wait, this is the easy part! Wait until…."

To be honest I'm not sure what she even said after that. All I heard was that this phase that I am so desperately trying to survive, that is putting me into real depression and destroying my identity is the easy part. I wanted to respond to her in anger and tell her, "Well… I guess you better take them with you now because I'm not going to survive this, I'm on my way home to throw myself off the deck." I wanted her to see my pain, I wanted her help, I wanted to strangle her. All at once I felt invisible. Her comments made me question everything about how hard this was for me. Was it me? Am I the issue here? Is this truly the easy part? Because that's unbearable. It was a small moment on my journey of motherhood, but it stuck with me for a really long time. Her words sent me deeper. She kicked me while I was down, instead of helping me in any meaningful way. Why? Why didn't she say nice things to me?

What would it look like if we only led with encouragement, instead of stating stressful things that you think are facts? Different moms have different personalities, and some struggle with early childhood while others struggle with the teenage years. Now don't get me wrong, it's all hard, being a parent. However, I believe some phases of life are more bearable than others. When a lady told me that she cherished the newborn phase, and that those were the easy parts, I felt so defeated. As a mom who is deeply, deeply struggling to just survive this phase, hearing that this was the easy part was downright terrifying. I felt as if I might as well end it now. If she had led with encouragement, if she would've known my personality - that I'm outdoorsy and love sports and love to help young kids through big emotions - she would've known that I would thrive with a child instead of a baby. She would've known that the baby part was the hardest part for me as a mother, and if I could just hold on and get to the toddler phase, that I was going to come into my own (and thrive) as a parent. She instead chose to take what she thought she knew and blanket it over me, causing me to feel completely hopeless and helpless and dumb in a time where I needed support the most.

We all have different personalities and skills and shortcomings, and that all translates into parenthood. It's not a one size fits all. You are going to struggle with the phases of life that highlight your shortcomings, and you are going to thrive in your child's life with the phases that align with your strengths. And that is different for everybody. Every child, every parent, everybody. Let's think before we speak. Lead with encouragement, because you don't get a badge for having it the hardest. You don't get a badge for letting a mother, who is so beat down and struggling, know that it only gets harder from there because you made it and you're on the other side. There is no trophy for the hardest life award. Why do we do that? Why can't we say, "Yeah, this is tough, and I see you. You are an incredible person and I know this phase is hard for you, but you are going to come into your own as a parent and become an incredible mother. It's just not your phase. You are going to thrive when your baby gets a little bit older." Or "You are going to thrive once the stress in your life eases out. That will happen for you, I just know it. Hold on, keep trying, you're doing great."

There will always be hurtful people in the world who just say the wrong things. Mamas, it is up to us to break that cycle. Encourage other moms and create a better world for ourselves. Karen's aren't going away, but we sure as heck aren't going to become them. Amen?

Chapter Twenty-Eight

Exist

The truth is… you get to exist.

I'm here to tell you some groundbreaking information that would have changed a lot for me in the early days of being a mom.

You get to exist. You get to have a personality, thoughts, dreams, goals, and friends. Let's not get carried away and think that life is still all about us, because honey, it's not. It's about the kids, and rightfully so. What I am saying is that although our roles change when we become moms and our world changes all around us, we still have the right to be a part of it.

I used to stress so bad about getting ready in the mornings. There wasn't anything I could do to help my little one who had colic stop crying. It's just part of the game, she would cry constantly. There were some days when I didn't even get to brush my teeth because I would be holding and taking care of her. I couldn't even meet my basic need of brushing my dang teeth. I felt like I wasn't being a good mom if I let her cry. I also felt like I didn't have a choice. I "couldn't" put her down.

What I didn't realize (and needed someone to tell me) was that it is a choice. It was a choice to choose myself, for two minutes. It wasn't going to scar my child or damage them past the point of no return. It truthfully wouldn't even bother them in the long run. I needed to be told that I was still a good mom if I just wanted a second to change my damn underwear.

Here is a secret, babies cry. A lot. It just happens, so don't let that stop you from existing. It is not a reflection of your worth as a mother. It is not a reflection of your parenting skills. I promise. It's just nature and science, babies cry. Put your baby down in a safe place and brush your dang teeth. You get to exist. Now, once again I must reiterate that I'm not advocating for an hour and a half of doing YouTube make-up tutorials whilst your younglings are screaming. I'm just saying, take two minutes and brush your teeth, brush your hair and for goodness' sake change your underwear mama.

Your needs are important too. You will be a better mom for it.

Chapter Twenty-Nine

You Earned It

The truth is... You've earned the right to choose.

I want you to know something. What I'm about to tell you is so liberating, it will change your life. Here it is. The minute that the adorable nine-pound meatball came out your va-jay-jay (or was cut out of the sunroof), you earned the right to choose whatever you want for your life. End of story.

Throughout my whole life I have always sought the counsel of adults. I always needed help with one thing or the other, and I begged them to tell me what to do. Then I would do it. I always took what my parents taught me as law, and I always strived to make them happy. Somewhere along the way that became my identity - a people pleaser. Let me tell you, it's exhausting. I'm a mom now, and it shouldn't feel like I'm not in control of my own life. It shouldn't feel as if other people are making all my decisions for me. Then why does it? The truth? I chose to feel this way. I let others dictate my decisions. I let others tell me what to do.

Growing up, I think it is wise for us to listen to our guardians. At some point, we become adults and start making our own choices. I must have missed the invitation to that boat because I was left so far behind, I can no longer even see it on the horizon. I must have missed where I was now a "grown up" and was supposed to make my own decisions. I became a people pleaser. Yuck. I took other people's advice as law and followed any direction I was given regardless of how I felt about it. I was afraid that people would see me as difficult or unruly. I was afraid to hurt people by telling them with my actions that I didn't like their idea. I just wanted to please.

This is how my life was until I became a mother.

As I was laying in the hospital bed after being cut open and a human body ripped from my loins, it hit me. I didn't have to let other people make my choices. I could make my own. I've earned it. I am officially an adult, I'm a mother.

Ready or not, it's time to put my big girl pants on (literally that hospital underwear is gigantic) and let some people down. I let the breastfeeding fanatics down because I only decided to breastfeed for four months for my own mental health. I let the fit mom group down because I had no interest in exercising for a long while, and the curves of my body showed that. I let careful moms down because I chose to bring my baby in public the first week home. So on and so forth. I made my choices, and I completely earned the right to.

When we become moms, everyone around us wants to share endless amounts of advice with us, welcomed or not. They tell us how to feed, how to heal, how to care, how to cope, how to keep friends, how to keep your marriage, how to do your hair, what to eat, who to read, where to go, and how to use the bathroom after birth. For goodness' sake people, I am a human being, not a robot! Slow down! I had to make a choice. Do I listen and follow? Or do I listen, assess, and make my own choice for what is best for my family? I chose the second, and I hope you do too. If you haven't looked at it this way before, and you are seeing things in a new light, I am so glad! It is never too late to start taking control over your own decisions and do what you think is right for your family. The truth is, you've earned it.

Chapter Thirty

Mirrors

The truth is... our children are our mirrors.

It was cleaning day. I had seven toys, two of my husband's cups, a paper plate, a blanket, a coat, and a half-eaten skittle that could choke my infant in my hands. My girls were playing in the living room while I buzzed around them in a fury. I was trying so hard to be efficient so we could all go on a walk after it was all picked up. I was hustling. One of the cups fell. A grunt so loud the neighbors could have heard it left my chest, and at the same moment my infant made some annoying noise and I shouted, "Oh stop!!" Not my finest moment as a mother.

A few days passed and I was sitting at my kitchen table working on some bills. My toddler had two baby dolls, one hairbrush, Buzz Lightyear, and a snack in her arms and she made her way to the rug to play. Poor buzz fell from her arms and hit the ground hard. She. Was. Upset.

She growled and shouted, "NOOOOO!" As if her life would end at that very moment. Her sister crawled fast to her fallen toy and gave Buzz a big hug. My oldest shouted at her though tears, "Stop it! Mine!". I was so discouraged. Why was she acting like this? I have taught her that things happen, and we roll with the troubles. In this house, we stay calm and figure out a solution together. Why is this her reaction?! I thought about it for a long time.

It was me. She's acting like me. I thought to myself, "Oh boy, what have I done?" *Do as I say, not as I do, young lady!* Now, I must give both of us a little grace because she's two and has no idea what that concept means and I'm a new mom and thus have no actual idea what I'm doing.

In the almost three years I've been a mother, I have noticed this mirroring concept over and over. No matter what I teach my girls, they see me and copy. They watch what I do and how I interact with the world around us. They adore me, I'm their mommy. They want to be like just like me, God love them. Although this is a sweet sentiment from the outside looking in, with it comes so much pressure.

I still have so much growing to do as a woman. I'm not even close to being perfected yet. Maybe that's why God gave me children. He knew I needed a little growth check. He gave me the opportunity with these little drama queens to become a better version of myself. Son of a gun, I don't want to. If you're anything like me, this reality check is heavy. This one hits a bit too close to home.

My girls see me. They copy me. They are me. If you are watching your kids and are sad about some of their behaviors, I challenge you to look at yourself and what they are seeing in you. They are probably copying you. How do we possibly fix that?! The answer is - we do our very best. Nothing short of that will do. I want us mamas to lay our heads down at the end of each night knowing we did our best. I want us to know that we did our best to model behaviors we want to see in our children. That we did our best in showing them how to interact with the people around us. Do our best to act how we want them to act. I also want them to know that if we fall short of the mark, that tomorrow is a new day, and we can try again. My dearest reader, I want you to know that you can do this. You can grow into a better version of yourself, and you can lead your children by example. God is calling you to it. It's going to be challenging, but if I can grow and be better, so can you mama.

Chapter Thirty-One

Choices

The truth is.... it's a choice.

It had been a rough start to the day. My littles were obscenely crabby and no matter what tactic I tried; they just couldn't pull it together. They were having an off day, and so was I. Things like that are a chain reaction in my home. If one person has negative energy, look out because now we all do. In typical mama fashion, I was in a complete tailspin. A bus could have taken out the entire left corner of my home, I didn't care. Nothing in these moments seems to matter to me. My give-a-rip is broken.

I struggled to get both girls dressed in cute outfits, because I'm a perfectionist. I made my way to my closet to climb the laundry mountain and picked something to put on my exhausted body. I was staring at my clothes and having an internal argument over what shirt has the less barf stains and would show my muffin top less. I heard behind me the dreaded infant burp/barf noise. I closed my eyes and just listened to the spit up hit the floor. I turned around and watched it ooze into the carpet and, before I could even make a move, my baby's hands were all up in it. It was her new favorite toy. Who am I to stop a good time? So, I sat down. I sat down in my closet. I had no more left in me. I couldn't even argue or fight or move. I just stopped and watched the spit up soak into my new carpet. After what seemed like 15 minutes, I stood up, got dressed and grabbed my girls. I put a dirty sock over the barf spot so I could deal with it later. I loaded the girls in the car and went and got coffee.

I could have made two choices right then and there. My first option would be to let the morning win. I could have fought against the oh-so-pressing fake clock in my brain and let the day go terribly. Or we could stop what we were doing and slow down. We need to look at the situation in front of us and take ourselves out of it for a moment.

As moms, we are often so close to the problem that it's hard to see on the other side. Once we step back, we can see that it's just an obstacle that has a solution. Our little ones look to us every day to set the tone. They look to us to see how to handle conflict and resolution. If I were to fly off the handle like every nerve in my body wanted me to (and like I have done so many times in the past), what would my girls see? Would they think that's how to handle a situation or an angry emotion?

When I am overwhelmed, angry, or any one of the host of emotions a mother deals with on the hourly, I stop what I'm doing and step back. I put my hands on my hips, take a deep breath and I think. I turn my anger into a challenge. How can I use what I know as a mom to overcome this situation? If I give my toddler a snack or a toy, she will stop screaming. If I pick my infant up, she stops screaming (most of the time). Then I have a quieter situation that I'm more equipped to handle. Babies screaming makes me want to Hulk-smash a broom over my knee. Yes, I know it probably wouldn't break and I'd leave one blueberry of a bruise, but it's worth a shot. Once I get the situation quiet, I can better deal with the problem.

Mamas, it's ok to step back. It's ok to put the kid down, take three steps backwards to give yourself space, and take a few deep breaths. This tactic has made a world of difference for me. It's been a game changer. It is up to us to set the tone of the day. Our littles need us. If you're like me and you fail on the daily and fly off the handle for no other reason than the anger of a thousand suns, it's ok. Forgive yourself, apologize, and move forward. Kiddos are so quick to forgive and forget, I love that about them. We all make mistakes, even the best of mamas. Do your best and when challenges arise, be aware that your littles are watching and learning from you. You can do this. It's a choice.

Chapter Thirty-Two

Comparison

The Truth is.... Comparison is poison.

I think us moms need to talk about something. It's not very fun, and most of us are extremely guilty. I know I am. One hundred percent. I want to talk about comparison. Ugh. Even saying it scares me. It is so common amongst moms today and it makes my heart sad. If society hasn't put enough pressure on us to raise perfect children, enter social media.

Everywhere we look there is a perfect mom doing her perfect lunges in her perfect home with her perfectly dressed perfect child strapped to her perfectly muscular back with the perfect carrier. Even typing that was exhausting. My goodness.

I like social media, don't get me wrong. I would probably even say that before having kids, I loved it. I love getting inspired and seeing new ideas and creating motivational home pages that help me grow. I could learn from others and use their successes and fitness plans to become a better version of myself. I get it, it can be inspirational for sure.

What happens when the things we are trying to achieve now as a mother don't have a clear path? No set plan that will get you to the finish line? What happens when everyone's plan does, and has to, look different from one another even though we are all succeeding? The answer is comparison. We take other mom's looks, ideas, and plans, and try to implement them into our own lives knowing dang well that our situation is different. When we fail at implementing it, we blame OURSELVES! WHAT? Do you see the absurdity in that?

Motherhood is not one size fits all, and that's an understatement. We are all unique. We have different bodies, hopes, homes, time schedules. We have different support and varying degrees of relationships. We make different amounts of money and live in different parts of the world. We participate in different cultural norms and go to different houses of worship. We think differently about how to parent and what is right and wrong. We feel differently about relationships with food and exercise. WE ARE DIFFERENT!! Why do we see a completely different woman on social media and think we want to be like her? It's nuts. In trying to be her, we completely lose the awesomeness of ourselves.

We are all unique for a reason. God made us exactly the way we are and exactly the way He wanted us. He gave us our personalities and our hearts. He gave us our families and led us through different experiences. He wanted us to be different on purpose. He made each one of us unique so that we WOULDN'T be like anyone else. Are you wanting to go toe-to-toe with the big guy upstairs? Probs not, mama.

Social media is a beautiful thing. It can be used for so much good. We can encourage others and get inspired. We can come together and build a support circle and make friends. But don't for one second let it take your uniqueness away. Stand strong and firm in exactly who you are. You never know who is looking at your posts wanting to be more like you. Your kids do not need a social media version of you. Your kids do not need a mom who is chasing some unattainable form of perfection. They need you. Simply you. The you that God created. Be her.

Chapter Thirty-Three

The Sun Will Rise

The truth is… the sun will rise tomorrow.

Through the pages of this book, you have seen my ups and downs. You have seen my triumphs and my most epic of #momfails. Looking back, I also recognize those moments in my own journey through motherhood. The drastic contrasts between success and failure happen often, even on the same day. The good times are good, but the hard times can be unbearable. One thing remains true throughout. No matter how incredible the #momwin was, or how bad of a day I had with my girls, the sun still rises the next morning. Time continues on.

I remember when my oldest daughter was a baby. She was such a hard baby to care for with her colic and extremely exuberant personality. She hardly slept in the first months at home, and it left me feeling lost and so alone in the long hours of the night. I remember thinking to myself, "what on earth have I done? Did I make a mistake? This is way too hard for me…" I cried a lot.

One night, she was sick with a 103-degree fever. She was miserable, which meant I was too. I knew I was in for a long night ahead of me, and my husband helped as much as he could. But he was holding down on the work front so we could have frivolous things like a home and food. I decided to let him sleep because I became accustomed to such things. He often was up all night with us, but this night I let him sleep, he needed it.

The sun set around 7:00 PM and we planted ourselves on the living room couch, but soon had to move to the nursery rocking chair because of the crying. There was no way my poor husband and his tender heart could sleep through it. We closed the door behind us and rocked. I rocked that fat potato for hours. About every hour of bouncing, shushing, walking, and rocking, she would close her eyes for about ten minutes. Our first home was a modest one, so her room was no bigger than 110 square feet. It was tiny. The path I walked was about three steps one way, then the other. Back and forth, until my body ached.

Somewhere around 2:00 AM I began to give up. I felt as if the morning would never come. I had done all I could and had taken all I could take. I felt stuck in a moment of time that felt cruel; a complete standstill. I didn't want to break and ask my husband for help, but I couldn't make it until morning.

These days were tough, they were slow and tedious and relentless. I wouldn't go back to those days for anything. I am so glad I am past that part of becoming a mommy.

The sun did indeed end up rising, and relief came when my mom walked through my front door and helped me take care of my little one. She encouraged me and loved me in a moment when I needed it most. I felt pride that morning. No matter how long it took to get there, I had done it. I had survived an endless night with a sick baby.

Years after these long nights, my baby turned into a toddler. She is the best. She's polite, kind, funny, and I must say, absolutely adorable. She is the light of my life. She brings joy and laughter wherever she goes.

We were headed to a family gathering for the 4th of July and I couldn't have been more excited! I was so excited to show my little girl off. I was proud of all the things she had learned, and I was proud (as a mom) that I helped her get there. I couldn't wait. It was a four-day vacation, and I was excited for each and every day.

As soon as we arrived, the compliments started coming. I was showered in admiration of how well she behaved and how smart she was. I was beaming. My little girl went to bed on time each and every night and woke up with a smile each morning. She loved her family members well and held hands with all her cousins. She killed it. Looking back, this is one of the proud mommy moments that I will forever hold on to. She and I had done it. We made our family proud. I wanted time to stand still and live in these moments.

The four days flew by in the blink of an eye, and before I knew it we were on our long journey home. How did that happen? I remember being so confused as to how that time went so fast compared to other moments in my life that seemed to take an eternity. It was unfair, really. I wanted these moments to last as long as the ones alone in my baby's nursery. I wanted time to drag on, enjoying every last second. But instead, it flew by without regard to my feelings or desires.

The thing is, no matter what you are going through, the sun still rises and sets the same way. No matter if moments are lasting as long as a dark night in the middle of despair or flying by like the moments of pure joy - the sun will still rise in the morning. It will still be one of my most favorite parts of God's creation and it will come whether you are ready for it or not.

Time is a funny thing, because it doesn't care about us. It doesn't care if you are young or old. It doesn't care whether you are a mom and struggling or if you are a grandma watching your last years pass by. It keeps going. In a weird way, I find comfort in that. I find comfort in knowing that this fact of life is completely out of my control. No matter what I do or how I'm feeling, the sun will still rise tomorrow morning.

Hang on. If during our hard moments we can hang on to the knowledge that the sun will still rise, it will give us great hope and encouragement that things will get better. If we can hold on during the moments that are pure bliss and seem to fly by in the blink of an eye, maybe we can savor them just a tiny bit longer, extending our joy just a bit further.

Know this mama, no matter your circumstance, the sun will

always rise in the morning, bringing with it hope, warmth, love, and one more try at making that day the best one yet.

Part Four:

Do

"Sometimes when we write these things down, they become more real. Dreams become achievable."

We have now grown together as mothers, and I have shared with you the tips and tricks that I have picked up along the way. I hope that you were able to relate to me, laugh with me, and grow as a mother with me. I hope you feel supported and loved. I also want you to know that you are an incredible mother in your own unique way, and there is no better way to be.

Now it's time for both of us to take the advice I often give to my toddler, "Less talkie, more walkie!!" It's time for us to saddle up and do the dang thing. This section of the book is a practical guide to all things mom. This section is comprised of fun activities for both mom and kiddos, some together, and some on your own. My heart for this section is to refresh your spirit by taking what I can off your plate. No need to come up with creative ideas on how to implement self-care or new and fun ideas for your kids. I've done the groundwork for you. You're welcome. These pages contain practical ways to act and to take responsibility for your growth. I'm not talking jean size here ladies - our hearts and soul need to grow as well. We need to get better; we need to constantly strive to be the best dang mothers for our kids that we possibly can be. It's hard to even know where to start, but I encourage you to finish this book with strength, motivation, and grace for yourself. We all have our shortcomings and irritations, but when we can be mindful about getting to know those things about ourselves, healing begins and generational traumas end. It starts with us. It starts with these activities. It starts with you. Go forth and DO.

Chapter Thirty-Four

Be The Joy

Have you ever thought about who thinks about you? I often do. I spend a lot of my days wondering how friends are doing and what they are up to. I do this not only with close friends that I'm still in contact with, but friends from long ago that I have just lost touch with. Who are they now? Where do they live? Have you ever seen the meme that reads, "Some of y'all never almost died in a corn field from way too much UV Vodka with your bestie, and it shows."? I did this exact scenario with friends named Rikki and Kristine, except it was on the lake in a blow-up raft. Those memories crack me up, and they feel like a lifetime ago. We are now all mothers to multiple children and have successful careers. I wonder if they ever think of that memory like I do? I wonder if they think of me? What would it look like if we all stopped wondering, put on our big girl pants, and reached out first? Be the joy in someone's day by letting them know you think of them. In my experience, the more random the memory or friendship, the funnier the response. The deeper the friendship, the more meaningful the response. Both responses are so fun and so needed.

Reach out to two friends today. Reach out via phone call, text, or on whatever social media platform suits you. Tell them you are thinking of them and are wondering what they are up to or how they are. Tell them they had an impact in your life, even if simply by a reoccurring memory. Who are you calling?

1.＿＿＿＿＿＿
2.＿＿＿＿＿＿

How did it go? What came up? Journal here about what feelings came up in you during this activity:

Chapter Thirty-Five

Who Are My People?

It is so important to know who our people are. There are many cheesy terms and phrases used to describe this group of people. My tribe, my homies, my village, my crew, my people. I love all of them. I don't mind which one you use during this activity, just insert your preferred term. Our true people are the few that know us deeply. They see past our knee-jerk reactions and know our true intentions. They are filled with unending grace and love. I think being a mother is one of the hardest and loneliest jobs on this planet. It takes every ounce of our being to get through most days. Our people lend us a shoulder when we need to cry, bring chocolate when we can't seem to make these kids listen, and sit with open ears and an open heart while we plan out our escape. And knowing deep down that we just needed to vent but we wouldn't want to be anywhere else but in our home.

This activity is designed to help us slow down, think, and put our thoughts to paper. Visually seeing things helps us process and understand. My hope for this exercise is that it does just that for you, as it has for me.

Community: People we see or talk to on a weekly or monthly basis. They are people we are friendly with and enjoy seeing. These people can be anyone from mom or dad to the nice lady at your favorite grocery store. Everyone you enjoy goes here. Breathe, think, write.

1._____   11._____
2._____   12._____
3._____   13._____
4._____   14._____
5._____   15._____
6._____   16._____
7._____   17._____
8._____   18._____
9._____   19._____
10._____   20._____

Love it. These people written above should make you smile. Now let's narrow it down. Who are your friends? Who can you tell an opinion to? Who can you share your parenting style with and receive encouragement? Who can you call when you get a flat tire? See where I'm going? Who are the people with a place at your dinner table?

1._____   6._____
2._____   7._____
3._____   8._____
4._____   9._____
5._____   10._____

Phew, that was harder. But you did it. You identified who is important to you, and who respects you. This last elimination will take some thought. This last group are your people. They are the ones who see past your outer image, right to the heart of you. They know you. They love your children as their own and vice versa. They are the family that you've created. These relationships are often mutual, as they are fulfilling, respectful, and easy. Take a deep breath and put your pen down, cross your arms if you must. Think of who holds the closest place to your heart? Who gets you? Who, my friend, are your people?

1. _____
2. _____
3. _____
4. _____
5. _____

There. You did it. These are the people that have a seat not only at your table but are invited to stay well after dinner is over. They are the most important people during your journey through motherhood. Having a friend like this is one of the most important things to have and to cherish. They are your sounding board and your outlet. Without them, let's be honest, we would go insane. It is also equally important to be all these things to them in return. If you filled these five spaces, you are very blessed. If your five spaces were empty, this is an opportunity for growth. Find your people and love them well, it truly makes all the difference.

Additional challenge: Send your five a text today explaining the activity and how and why you value them.

Chapter Thirty-Six

Moments

What do your moments look like with your child? Do they look funny and full of life and laughter? Do they look controlling and structured without room for give? Do they look sad, full of tears and loneliness? What moments are shaping your child's day?

How can we change every moment to one full of joy and laughter? We can't. Sorry, that's wildly unrealistic. What we can do is change some. Let's strive for progress. Let's start with one moment.

Write down a less than perfect moment from yesterday.

_____

_____

_____

_____

_____

What were your emotions? Why was it hard?

_____

_____

_____

_____

_____

Often times, we just need a second to regroup. In this tough moment, could you take a physical step back and take a deep breath? Could you slow down the schedule in your head that your kid knows nothing about, and relieve the pressure? Could you clap your hands four times, cover your eyes, do a circle, and hop once to reset your stamina of keeping it together? What actual physical action will help you stay calm and focused? Hint: The answer is not to give up caring and let anything and everything slide. The answer is to acknowledge these hard moments and come up with a strategy to help us grow strong enough to conquer them with grace and laughter.

What action can you do when things are ready to explode, to settle your heart down? What helps calm you?

_____

_____

_____

_____

_____

_____

_____

_____

Go forth and put this into action. Watch those hard moments become less aggressive over time. Watch yourself grow into a mom who can keep her cool and laugh with her children during a hysterically funny hard moment. You can do this; it takes practice… and a bit of humor.

Chapter Thirty-Seven

Have Some Fun!!

If you're like me, we often forget how to have fun with our kids. We get stuck in a routine that is mundane and stale. In our routine we somehow become out of touch with things that are FUN!! Below is a list of activities. Some are messy, some are probably a bad idea, and all of them are LOTS OF FUN!! Pick a few and do them with your kids. Don't forget to take pictures because these are the moments we need to remember and cherish.

Bathtub Mayhem: put your kid in the bathtub, fully clothed, with tons of waterproof toys. Without giving an explanation or any instructions, turn the water on. Let the funny memories begin. (Clean-up tip: Undress them when they are ready to be done, get them out of the bath and dressed. Address the mess after everyone is dry, calm, and relaxed.)

Painter: Fill a bucket with shaving cream or cool whip. Give your kiddo a paint brush and the bucket and let them go ham outside on the patio (wash off with hose) or inside at the kitchen table.

Blackout: Create an obstacle course either inside or outside depending on weather. Include a kitchen chair obstacle, a jump rope, over and under structures, balance activity and motion stations. Motions can be jumping jacks, push-ups, spins, crab walk etc. Show your child the course, turn on some music, and put a blindfold on them!! Either you, a sibling, or a friend guides them through the course. It's so fun!!

No Hands: Sit your child at a completely clean kitchen table in a long-sleeved shirt. Put a mask over their eyes, have them take their arms out of their sleeves and tie the empty sleeves behind them. When they are blindfolded, you put snacks on the table. Make it fun by adding snacks that are hard to eat without hands. Snack packs, Jell-O, crackers, fruit, veggies, mashed potatoes, whip cream, etc. Take the mask off and instruct them to eat whatever they want, but NO HANDS! (Pro tip: use entire table, it's way messier, and way more fun.)

Nose Hands: This activity is the best with multiples. If you have an only child, you may have to play. Put a $1, $5, or $10 bill against the wall. Have your kids put their hands in their back pockets or behind their backs. Hold the bill to the wall with their nose. Whoever stays the longest wins the money! Play a few rounds.

Go. To. The. Park. (Mom tip: Google parks in your surrounding area and go to one you've never been to before.)

Rock Band: Set up drum stations with bowls, cans and utensils. Put on some music and jam out. It's more fun with more random items. Boxes, cans, toys, an old tire, sticks, etc.

Photoshoot: Teach your kiddo to use a camera, either disposable or on your phone. Then set up a funny scene with their help and let them take your picture!! Print their pictures of you, even if they are terrible, and hang them on the fridge for everyone to see.

Name game: At the kitchen table, place a blank piece of paper in front of your child. Open the marker of the color they choose, put it in their mouth and instruct them to write their name! (Tip: put newspaper or another sheet of paper under their paper so the marker doesn't ruin your kitchen table.)

Handshake: Create a secret family handshake. The wackier the better! Do a spin, a jump, and a roll if you have to. Let the kids lead the way on this one. You can do this handshake anywhere and it really creates a special exclusive safe moment for your family.

Bake off: As a family, bake a delicious treat that can be decorated. If you are not a baker, this can be a fun opportunity to try something new in front of your kids to teach them its ok to not be good at everything. It's ok, I promise. Once baked, it's time to let the creativity shine. Set out gummy bears and skittles, Oreos, and milk duds. Set it all out and decorate. Take pictures of all the beautiful creations. Send them to family members for a game of Who Made What if you're brave!

Glue It: Get each child, and yourself, a poster board and a bottle of glue and head to a park. Also, bring all of the wet wipes. Set out the poster boards and glue on a sidewalk, set boundaries, and say go. Let each kid find what they want, when they want, and how they want, and let them glue anything to their board. If they want to attempt to glue a rock, let them. Let them learn through exploration that the rock is too heavy to stick. Catch my drift? Let those kids learn through play that some things work, and some don't. Some things look cool, some don't. Have fun and display in your backyard or spare room for a week when it's all done. What. A. Masterpiece. And what a fun memory. Did I mention, don't forget to take pictures!!

Where does this go?: Collect items around the house ahead of time in a basket. Think a single sock, a watch, a toothbrush, a spoon, a remote etc. Sit in the main room of your home and have the kids find the items spot. Teach them that everything has a spot. Help the little ones complete the task. If your kids are a bit older, time them to see how fast they are. Bonus points if you record their time on a piece of paper. (Tip: pick a few funny things like their underpants or dad's smelly sock.)

Chapter Thirty-Eight

Let's List

Being a mom means often having a jumbled brain. Somewhere along the line, it became a mom's job to keep track of literally everything in life, whether she works in the home, at an office, or not at all. It's the mom's job to keep it all straight. It means keeping track of soccer practice, band instruments, grades, and friends. It's where your partner is and what their schedule is. Who needs to be picked up and where. It's trying to remember what needs to be cleaned and how long that food spot has been on the floor. It's a lot. All the time. It requires that we become a real-life superhero of the mind. Let's take a minute and get all of that out of your brain. Let's purge. Let's word vomit. Let's list.

Write down everything that needs to be done in the near future so you can see it on paper and make a plan. Write it down so your brain can be free, even if just for a moment. After it is all written down, rip this page out of this here book and slap it on the fridge. Slap it on there for no other reason so that others can see the tasks you do, because you deserve to be noticed mama.

To-Do:

_____

_____

_____

_____

_____

_____

Chapter Thirty-Nine

Relax!!

Are you modeling relaxation to your children? Do they know how? Do they know it's necessary to slow their bodies down? Don't get me wrong, kids don't do well at this activity, and I am well aware of their inability to sit still. What if we practiced this skill with them? I challenge you to slow down and be quiet with your kids every day.

This skill can greatly help your child in the future. The ability to sit in stillness can improve your child's ability to stay on task, control their arousal level, and it can help them better control their emotions. That all sounds like a win to me.

Activity:

Sit on the floor in a low-lit room. Face your child as you both sit crisscross applesauce, hands in lap. Have a relaxing, non-lyric, song playing softly. Teach them how to be still. Phrases such as "freeze" or "don't move" trigger a muscle response, so try not to use them. Instead, explain what a calm body feels like in a calm tone of voice. Help them learn how to take deep breaths. The first few times of doing this activity will be very active and hands on, but over time they will learn to be still. Start with no talking, no moving, and eyes open or shut for two minutes. As they progress in this skill, increase the time. As they become restless, acknowledge the activity is over and they did a good job, even if they are still learning. (Note: if laying on your back works better for you, that is totally okay. These activities are yours to try with your family, adapt as needed.)

Chapter Forty

Let's Journal

As a mother, our minds and hearts are always pulled in a thousand different directions. We are asked to do so much throughout our days for a million different people. Rarely are we asked how we are doing. So here I am, as a friend, checking in on you.

How are you doing? No, really. How are you doing? What if we could tell the truth to this question? How liberating would that be? In the space below, let it all out. No one will see what you write, and no one will judge you. If you hate something, write it down. Failing? Write it down. Angry? Write it down. Succeeding in an area? Write. It. Down.

The following page provides the space for you, my dear friend, to do nothing but write. Don't worry about punctuation or mistakes. This is for you. This is to get all the inside thoughts, out.

How are you?

_____
_____
_____
_____
_____
_____
_____
_____
_____
_____
_____
_____
_____
_____
_____
_____
_____
_____
_____
_____
_____
_____
_____
_____
_____
_____
_____
_____
_____

Now rip this page out of this book, tear it into a thousand pieces and throw it away. Just so nobody sees it because let's be honest, kids are nosey. Unless it's your choice to share with those around you, which I highly encourage.

Chapter Forty-One

Dream Board

I'm a dreamer. I always have been. I'm not talking about a daydreamer, but a real dreamer about things I want to come to fruition in my life. I chase after my dreams with everything I have. Case in point, this published book. I have always wanted to write a book, to impact others, and to leave a legacy for my daughters. I wanted to give women across the country a friend. I wrote my goal on a sheet of paper and circled it. Around that circle I wrote down all the ways I could make that happen. I wrote down what steps to start with and how to grow little by little until my dream was a reality. In the bottom corner of my page, I documented the top three challenges that would need work, so they don't stand in the way of my goal. Mine were money, time, and resources. I knocked those challenges out one-by-one. I saved money until I had enough, I set aside time on a weekly basis to write, and I asked anyone I knew how to get published as well as a few thousand google searches. Over time, my challenges were nonexistent, and my dream started to come together. Sometimes when we write these things down, they become more real. Dreams become achievable.

What is your dream? What are the steps to reach it? What are the challenges?

Steps:

1._____   6._____
2._____   7._____
3._____   8._____
4._____   9._____
5._____   10._____

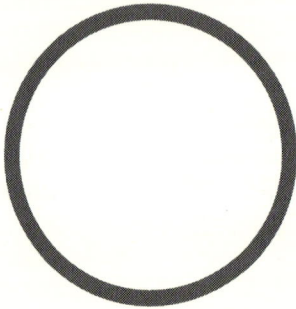

You CAN do this

Challenges:

1._____
2._____
3._____

Chapter Forty-Two

Self-Care Bingo

This is blackout Bingo my friend! Go get a gift card to your favorite place, or a cash bill as a prize and put it up on the fridge so you see it every day. Pro tip: read all the challenges first. Many take planning, especially as a mother. You can do this.

Here are the rules:

You must get a blackout Bingo in 30 days

If you fail to get a blackout, you need to give your prize to a friend, and try again.

Bonus: add a gift for your spouse, so they help you win. It's a win, win.

Go girl, go.

TRY YOGA (ONLINE OR IN PERSON)	GO FOR A WALK OR RUN	GIVE OR RECEIVE A 30 SECOND HUG	FINISH THIS BOOK
DANCE TO FAVORITE 3 SONGS IN A ROW	GO TO BED AN HOUR EARLY WITHOUT YOUR DEVICE	CALL A FRIEND OUT OF THE BLUE	GO FIND A ROCK, PAINT IT, AND LEAVE SOMEWHERE RANDOM
STRETCH FOR 20 MINUTES	GET COFFEE OR LUNCH WITH A FRIEND	WRITE SOMEONE A LETTER AND PHYSICALLY MAIL IT	CLEAN YOUR HOUSE
BUY SOMETHING FOR YOURSELF	LISTEN TO A FREE PODCAST WITHOUT INTERRUPTION	TAKE A SELFIE THAT YOU LIKE	COOK A HEALTHY MEAL

Chapter Forty-Three

Phone Free!

Challenge time. I often feel pulled in twenty-two different directions. I am trying to care for my kids while simultaneously answering texts, emails, social media posts, and an actual phone call. My attention is constantly pulled in a thousand directions. One of the main distractions that pulls me away from focusing on my kids is my phone. It demands my attention. My phone is like this magnet that is constantly pulling me towards it, even though I know I should be present exactly where I am. Here's the challenge. Be phone free for 24 hours. Completely. Have the phone in the home on a loud ringer setting just in case of emergency but leave it alone. Do not touch it, do not look at it, don't even think about it. Wake up, go about your day, and be present. Also, it may be a smart idea to let loved ones and besties know that you will be phone free that day, so they don't call the police! Other emails, texts, posts, and anything the like can wait. Can you do it?

After: How did that feel? What did you learn? Want to do it again? Why?

_____

_____

_____

_____

_____

_____

_____

Chapter Forty-Four

Let's Journal... Again

So often I find myself asked to describe a friend. I love this! I get to explain why I love someone. I love describing who they are, how they act, what they love, where they work, and so on. I like introducing people to others because I often go above and beyond and add fun details about them in my description. This always catches people by surprise, and I love to see the joy on their face when they hear how awesome I think they are.

How would you describe yourself? If you were someone else introducing you to another person. What would you say? Who are you? What are you like? What's your vibe? What's important for others to know about you? What makes you, you?

_____

_____

_____

_____

_____

_____

_____

Conclusion

I can't believe I finished this project. Wow. This book started as a thought that turned into a dream, that turned into a project, that turned into one of the greatest achievements of my life. Over the past two years, I have poured my heart and soul into this project. I have spent countless hours writing, crying, and learning. I sat for long hours of the night at my desk after my two babies went to sleep, trying to put into words what had happened to me that day. I have scoured the deepest depths of my memories and my emotions and put everything that I have found on the page in the most vulnerable way that I could. I have the deepest hope in my heart that you enjoyed this book as much as I enjoyed creating it. Creating this book changed me. In the process of trying to find more content, it made me slow down and see the events and funny moments before me. It made me be present, and I am forever grateful for that. If I hadn't been writing this book for the two first years of being a mom, I'm pretty confident I would have gone crazy or worse, missed beautiful funny moments in the life of my girls.

Like I said in the beginning of this book, the thought of moms feeling alone with nowhere to turn or without a mom friend kept me up at night. It rocked me to my core. As an empath, it greatly disturbed my heart. I couldn't just continue in this world knowing that there are moms out there struggling and I did nothing to help. I hope in reading my book you found a friend, that you found someone you can relate to, someone you can laugh with, and someone you can grow with. I hope we can both take what we have learned in these pages and go forward and be awesome mamas!

These pages serve as a reminder for me as to how far I have

come. A reminder of all the things that have come before and of all the things that I'm sure will come to pass. I continue to read through these chapters over and over to relearn lessons and to get motivated once again to be a mom. I invite you to do the same. The lessons in this book will never grow stale or outdated. The chapters are a timeless look at the many obstacles of being a mother, with a little humor of course!

Thank you for letting me share my heart with you. Thank you for opening your eyes, ears and heart to my family and our experiences. Thank you for receiving me with grace in all of my mess!

I genuinely hope that we can meet one day. I hope that my words and experiences have touched a place in your heart so special that you want to share that same experience with others. I would love to be a part of all women's journeys into (and through) motherhood. I want to come alongside all the beautiful women out there and create a community of genuine friendships. I hope to continue to inspire others by sharing this book through private events, public speaking, and everything in between. I want to continue this journey! If this is something you would like to partner with me in, please reach out via my website hannahmadsen.net. I would LOVE to meet you!

As the days continue to come and go and we continue to grow into the big shoes that mothers before us left, let us remember how incredible the process is. It is not always about the finish line when being a mom, it's about the mundane, day to day moments. It's about all the moments you wish you were stronger, the moments that test you, and the ones that strengthen you. Motherhood is about the moments that bring you immense joy and deep sadness, moments that bring you chaos and peace. It's about being completely present in these moments and living in two polar opposite worlds at the same time while navigating growth with a baby strapped to your boob. It's hard. It's incredible. Motherhood is made in moments and all of those moments are the real moments that truly make a mother.

Acknowledgements

To be an author has been a dream I harbored in my heart for most of my life. I always knew it would take a village to get me here, but little did I know just how important that village would become to me. I have many people to thank.

Shawn Madsen. Thank you for giving me encouragement each and every day to continue when it seemed impossible. Thank you for asking questions and talking about memories to inspire the chapters written in this book. Your love, laughter, and constant support has given me the space needed to achieve my dream. Thank you.

Scott and Barbara Berndt. The people that made me. My parents. I am who I am today because of you. You have never failed to support me. You two have always pushed me to be the best version of myself and have always made sure that humble morals stay at the center of my heart. Although a tall order, I strive to be like you, both individually, on a daily basis. You continuously help me with my kids, and for that I don't have meaningful enough words. Without you, this book would have never seen a shelf. Thank you.

Codie Winslow and CW Publishing. Codie, if not for your encouragement and gentle kick in the rear, my project would never have started. You made this happen for me and I will be forever grateful. CW Publishing, thank you for taking a chance on a small-town, first-time writer. You allowed me a platform to publish, and to achieve my goals. My dream became a reality because of you. Thank you.

Andie Anderson. My writer friend. Thank you for the endless inspiration and encouragement. Your words always hit the paper with

. such elegance, and I fan girl over your writing every time I get the opportunity to read or hear it. I value your thoughts and experience more than you know. Thank you.

My tribe. The women who supported me with laughs, late night phone calls, tears, ladies' nights out, and so much more. You women are all top notch and will always have a deep place in my heart. Jeana Sayler, Taylor White, Amber Muller, Crystal Lowry, Megan Loiacano, Stacey Schuck, and my entire MOPS crew. You women save me daily. Thank you.

Keri Bolduan. My family. Thank you for gifting me the notebook that held all the random thoughts that created this book. Your gift will always be cherished, and you will always be thought of and appreciated. Thank you.

Thank you to every person who has in any way assisted in this journey. There are undoubtedly many people left unnamed who have helped me reach the top of this mountain. I am forever grateful and sincerely hope I have the opportunity to someday pay it forward. Thank you.

About the Author

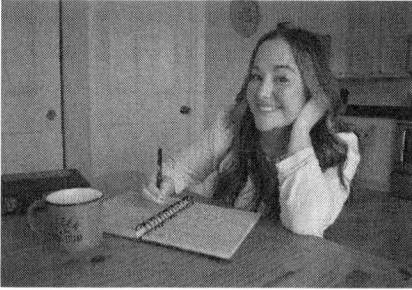

Hannah Madsen is on a mission to help Moms realize they are not alone. Her blog, about the modern-day struggles of motherhood, invites readers to come as they are. She is also a sought-after public speaker, social media personality, and MOPS Coordinator. She is a wife of 5 years and mother of 2. She invites readers into a real look at motherhood. She and her family make their home in Colorado. She blogs at HannahMadsen.net.

Hannah Jayde Madsen

Hannahjmadsen

Hannahjmadsen

hannahjaydemadsen

Made in the USA
Middletown, DE
17 November 2022